This book

23. NOV. 198 th

RURAL ANGLICANISM
a future for young Christians?

RURAL ANGLICANISM

a future for young Christians?

Leslie J. Francis

Research Officer, Culham College Institute for Church Related Education

Collins

Collins Liturgical Publications
187 Piccadilly, London W1V 9DA

Distributed in Ireland by
Educational Company of Ireland
1 Talbot Street, Dublin 1

Collins Liturgical Australia
P.O. Box 3023, Sydney 2001

Data capture by Culham College Institute for Church Related Education
Phototypeset by Burgess & Son (Abingdon) Ltd
Printed by William Collins Sons & Co, Glasgow

CONTENTS

PREFACE
by His Grace the Archbishop of Canterbury

Dr Francis has written a timely, and devastating book. In it he documents not only the statistical demise of rural Anglicanism, but also the degree to which it no longer reflects its Barsetshire caricature. His research clearly demonstrates that the countryside is now as much a pastoral challenge to today's Church as the inner city. How, he asks, *does* rural Anglicanism successfully proclaim the Gospel of Christ, and what kind of spirituality *is* the Church able to offer those communities it was once designed to serve?

Such leading questions are often fudged or forgotten. Dr Francis argues that they must be met not only by more effective use of manpower and resources, but also by specific pastoral strategies aimed at the rural young. I welcome this particular emphasis. If the Victorian country clergy rightly feared the alienation of the poor from their Church, their successors must recognise the alienation of today's young from theirs. Christian education and Church-based Youth Work are vital here, as well as more direct Church concern with unemployment among rural school-leavers.

Dr Francis' study is scrupulously researched and clearly presented, and buttressed by vivid case studies as well as statistics. It is a refreshing contrast to some of the blander and more theoretical writing currently available on pastoral issues. As such it deserves the widest possible readership and discussion.

Robert Cantuar
25 January 1985

FOREWORD

This study brings together my three professional interests in religion, education and social science research. It stems from my deep conviction that the churches can benefit from employing the research methods of the social sciences in order to see more clearly the nature, the scope and the limitations of their impact on contemporary society. The present focus on rural Anglicanism is one particularly close to my own heart, since I exercise my own non-stipendiary ministry in a rural diocese. A great number of changes are taking place in rural dioceses: I hope that this study will prove to be useful both in evaluating the present situation and in planning for the future.

The aim of this study has been to uncover new information about the nature and the extent of the contact which rural Anglican churches are currently making with their parishioners and especially with young people. This aim has required the systematic gathering of a great deal of quantitative and qualitative data. Social science research of this nature is both an expensive and a time consuming activity. I am, therefore, particularly grateful to the three bodies which, in their different ways, helped to generate, finance and sustain this piece of work.

First, the main survey discussed in this study was conducted under the auspices of the Diocesan Education Committee, as a major contribution to the promotion of its concern in the diocese with education. The Diocesan Education Committee gave considerable care to debating the aims and objectives of such a survey, to considering the design of the questionnaire used in the of such a survey, to considering the design of the questionnaire used in the survey and to assessing the practical application of the information discovered by the exercise. Members of the Diocesan Education Committee, together with other volunteers from the deaneries, gave freely of their own time in personally distributing the questionnaires and in assuring the most remarkably high response rate. Much of the initiative and enthusiasm inspiring this survey came from the Reverend Gareth Morgan and Ms Natasha Schemanoff. The Reverend Boyd Wesley also offered valuable assistance at various stages of the project.

Second, the smaller survey discussed in this book was conducted with the help of students from Westcott House, Cambridge, as a result of a seminar I was invited to conduct there by the vice-principal, the Reverend Dr John Armson.

Third, the full and detailed analysis of the data collected through these two surveys was made possible by the interest of the Reverend Dr John Gay, director of the Culham College Institute for Church Related Education, and by the generosity of that foundation in making available funding for the employment of a temporary research assistant and a part-time secretary. The work of research assistant was undertaken with skill and insight by Nicola Slee, to whose credit much of the following report must be attributed.

My thanks are also due to a number of other people who have helped to organise the data, commented on various drafts of the manuscript and encouraged its completion, especially to Andrew Bowden, Peter Brierley, Sue Chapman, Alan Davies, Douglas Fryer, Eddie Gibbs, Geoffrey Blackwell, Graham Howes, Valerie Moore, Judith Muskett, Margaret Wickham, Christine Wright and Mervyn Wilson. I am also grateful to Carole Boorman who typed the original draft of this study, and to Clare Gowing and Kim Luckett who prepared the final manuscript for printing.

The statistics displayed in Tables 2.1 through 2.5, and incorporated in the discussion of historical trends in chapter two, are derived from various editions of *The Church of England Year Book* and the Statistical Supplements to the year book. I am grateful to Robin Brookes of Church Information Office Publishing and to the Central Board of Finance for permission to draw on these statistics.

In order to study contemporary rural Anglicanism in depth, I have focused the research on just one diocese. After much thought and discussion I have decided not to name the diocese, since I believe that the patterns identified in this diocese are generally reflected much more widely throughout the rural church. I must also emphasise that, while the descriptions of parishes, churches and clergy in chapters ten and twelve are based totally on fact, the names attributed both to the places and the people are fictitious and not identifiable through *Crockford's Clerical Directory*.

One of the main theses of this study is that an important index of the health of rural Anglicanism is the contact which the churches in a rural diocese have with young people. Such an index points not only to the strength of the rural churches today, but to their likely strength in the future. The overall picture which emerges from the study is one from which the church can take little comfort. Rural Anglicanism seems to be cutting very little ice among young people today. Such a conclusion can be seen either as a cause for depression or as a springboard for challenge. Either way, it firmly dispels any notion we may cherish that all is well with the Church of England in a rural setting. The time is right for the rural Anglican church to re-evaluate its priorities and to re-design its strategies if it is going to make a significant impact on young people in rural areas during the last part of the twentieth century.

Culham College Institute,   Leslie J. Francis
November 1984

1 INTRODUCTION

There is a popular notion that the strength of the Anglican church lies in the rural parts of England, and there is some truth in that notion. Historically the Church of England has been well placed to give pastoral care to the rural community and to nurture the rural population in the Anglican faith. After all, it is basically here that the historic churches, parsonages and endowments have provided the essential framework through which the clergy of the Church of England have been enabled to function, whether or not they have made best use of that opportunity.

To the casual observer the strength of rural Anglicanism may well seem to remain largely unchanged. The holiday-maker to East Anglia, the West Country or the Lake District may well feel that things today look much as they did thirty years ago. Each rural community still possesses its Anglican church, and many of these communities still look to the Anglican church as their crowning architectural glory, as well as one of their major tourist attractions.

The more assiduous student of the English countryside may well go armed with one of the famous guides to the architecture and character of the counties of England. The first volume in Nikolaus Pevsner's *The Buildings of England* appeared in 1951, while Arther Mee's classic series *The King's England* dates from before the second world war. The point is that both series are still accurate guides to the architectural beauty of rural Anglicanism. At this level little has changed. If the preservation of its church buildings is an indication of the strength of rural Anglicanism, the Church of England seems to be maintaining its position very well, especially when comparison is made with the number of closed, demolished, converted or decaying chapels which point so poignantly to the decline of the rural Free Churches.

It is true that every so often the persistent visitor who aims to track down even the most out-of-the-way churches comes across the surprise of a redundant, derelict, decaying or even converted Anglican church. In fact, in the diocese in which the present study is based, as many as thirty-seven churches have been declared redundant, either wholly or in part, between the introduction of the Pastoral Measure, 1968, and 1984. Nevertheless, none of these churches has actually been demolished, and in the majority of cases the visitor could be forgiven for failing to notice the change of status.

Once the tourist begins to raise his or her head from the architectural guide books and begins to question in more depth the health of rural Anglicanism, a less comfortable picture begins to emerge. Perhaps tourists first ask questions when they find that the church is locked, concealing from their eyes the secrets and glories of its Norman font. Perhaps there is no notice telling them where to obtain the key, so they set off to find the rector in the house next door. While the rectory remains, the visitors soon learn that it has been sold and that the locked church has no resident incumbent. Perhaps on the way to find the churchwarden's house and to ask for the key there, the visitors pass the disused Church of England school, now prettily converted to a country cottage. At the churchwarden's house, they begin to learn how the regular pattern of two or three Sunday services, which was maintained until only ten or fifteen years ago, has now been reduced to a fortnightly late morning Communion and a mid-afternoon Evensong on the fifth Sunday of the month. They may then begin to wonder what kind of spirituality this church is able to offer to the community it was once built to serve and still continues to dominate by its Gothic architectural presence.

Behind the unchanging facade of the church building itself, rural Anglicanism has been undergoing a massive upheaval during the past twenty years. Certainly there have been cultural, educational and social changes taking place among the kind of people who live in rural areas. The process of secularisation is taking its toll even in rural England, where there is a growing movement away from what the churches stand for and an increasing lack of sympathy with what the churches are doing. Rural Anglicanism is proclaiming the gospel of Christ in an increasingly difficult market place.

. The problems faced by rural Anglicanism during the past twenty years have been greatly compounded by the sharp decrease in the resources available to it. Pressures to contract have come from three main sources. First, in an inflationary economic situation, the real value of invested and historic income has been seriously eroded. The consequence is that less money has been available for the payment of full-time stipendiary clergy. The parishes have been encouraged to raise more towards payment of their clergy. Benefices have been amalgamated in order to economise on stipends. Property assets in the form of parsonage houses have been sold.

Second, the number of men presenting themselves and being

accepted for ordination training has failed to keep pace with the vacancies being created through retirement. Meanwhile, the crisis of manpower has been mounting as more and more of the Anglican clergy move towards retirement age. The development of training and deployment of the non-stipendiary ministry has not met the gaps produced by the decline in the stipendiary ministry. By continuing to hold out against the ordination of women to the priesthood, the Church of England has deprived itself of considerable additional human resources.

Third, since the publication of the *Sheffield Report* in 1974, the deployment policy of the Church of England has been to 'encourage the most effective distribution of a diminishing number of clergy over the country as a whole'. The concept of the most effective use of manpower has been understood to involve 'fairer shares as between dioceses than the existing distribution, based on historical patterns rather than present needs, provided'. The consequences of the implementation of the Sheffield proposals has inevitably meant the planned running down of stipendiary clerical manpower in rural dioceses.

My aim in this book is neither to lament nor to criticise the changes that are taking place in rural Anglicanism. As a researcher and as a social scientist what I propose to do is to look in as much detail as possible at the changes that are taking place. I believe that this kind of study is necessary to help the church to see at a practical level the consequences of social, economic and administrative changes. Then, as a parish priest working in a rural diocese, I propose to reflect on the information made available by my research. I want to undertake this work both as a researcher and as a priest because I believe that rural Anglicanism has reached an important crisis in its development, a crisis from which it can emerge either much strengthened or seriously weakened.

It is true that a lot can be learnt by casual and careful observation, but what an impartial researcher tries to do is to be more systematic and accurate in his collection of information. The substance of this book brings together three such systematic research exercises.

All of the three research projects are based on just one diocese, the same diocese in each case. There are both strengths and weaknesses in limiting a study in this way. The strength is that rural Anglicanism in this limited geographical area can be studied in considerable depth. The weakness is that the results may or may not be typical of what could be found in other rural dioceses. My own conviction is that the strength far outweighs the weakness. By looking in depth at what is happening in just one diocese research can begin to provide us with a wealth of insights into what is happening elsewhere. Ideally such an analysis will act as a challenge for other researchers to tackle similar studies in other places and to begin to demonstrate just how their dioceses differ from the one described in my study. At present, the plain truth of the matter is that there are insufficient resources available to researchers to enable them to carry out the kind of independent enquiry I have undertaken here over a wider geographical area.

The first of my research exercises occupies just chapter two. This is a project based on the methods used by the statistically minded historian. I was intrigued to find out just how the statistical strength of rural Anglicanism in this one diocese had changed over recent years. The historian is seriously restricted by the nature of the statistical information that has been collected at different points in time and preserved. Since the mid-1950s, The *Church of England Year Book* has published fairly consistent tables of statistics charting various aspects of church membership. Additional information has been available from diocesan records and the county archives. By bringing together information published previously in different places I began to be able to assemble several reliable indices of the way in which the strength of rural Anglicanism has been changing during the past thirty years.

The information discussed in chapter two is, however, severely limited in its scope for the simple reason that the statistics regularly collected by the Church of England only cover a narrow range of aspects of church life. These kinds of statistics, which this chapter discusses, are the electoral roll figures, the Christmas and Easter communicants, baptisms, confirmations, and the number of clergy and licensed readers. In order to give some perspective to these figures they are set in the context of the changing number of people actually living in the diocese.

The second of my research exercises occupies a much larger portion of this book, chapters three through ten. Because the kind of statistical information I wanted did not already exist, I had to set out to collect it. What I wanted to do was to provide an accurate picture of the contact currently made by the churches in this rural Anglican diocese with their parishioners. I wanted to know how many services were conducted on a Sunday, what kind of services they were, when they took place and how many people came to them. In particular I wanted to look in greater detail at the contact made by the churches in this rural Anglican diocese with young people, those aged twenty-one years and younger. It seemed to me that this was a particularly powerful test both of the present strength of rural Anglicanism and of its prospects for the future.

The way I set about collecting this kind of information was through the design of a short questionnaire which was personally distributed to every clergyman in the diocese who was in charge of a benefice. Chapter three provides the background information and the technical details necessary in order to assess the results of this survey. This chapter discusses the design of the questionnaire, the sampling strategy and the response rate. The personal distribution of the questionnaire assured the remarkably high response rate of 92.4%. This makes the replies to the questionnaire truly representative of the diocese from which they are drawn.

The replies to this questionnaire made available a lot of unique information about what is taking place in rural Anglicanism today. The information is worth analysing from a number of different perspectives. In chapter four, an overall view is given of the total contact in this rural Anglican diocese between the churches and their parishioners, giving special attention to the contact with young people aged twenty-one and under. Then chapter five looks in much greater detail at what is taking place in the regular pattern of Sunday services themselves. It looks at the times and forms of services used in the churches and analyses the number of people who attend them. In particular, this chapter focuses attention on the pattern of church-going among young people. For example, I wanted to know the proportion of Sunday services which actually have young people present at them, as well as the number and age structure of young church attenders. I was curious to know whether there were particular forms of service and particular times of day when young people were more likely to be in church.

Chapter six moves attention from the Sunday services to the other provisions through which the local churches have contact with young people. It analyses the impact of Sunday schools, youth clubs, pathfinders and CYFA, church sponsored uniformed organisations, including cubs and scouts, brownies and guides, and the boys brigade, the church lads and church girls brigade, confirmation classes, house groups, bell ringers, choirs and choir practices, servers and membership of the parochial church council. For example, I wanted to know what proportion of the benefices actually operated Sunday schools, how many young people came to these Sunday schools and for which ages Sunday schools tended to cater. At another level, I was curious to know the extent to which the art of bell ringing was still able to recruit young ringers into the towers of the rural Anglican churches.

Chapter seven examines how the clergy in this rural diocese exercise their ministry among young people in ways not already dealt with in the previous chapter. The three main areas looked at are through schools, through the uniformed organisations which are not necessarily church sponsored and through interdenominational and secular youth work. For example, I wanted to know the extent to which the rural Anglican clergy can be regarded as a 'presence' in their community through their contact with schools. I was curious to know how regularly they are invited or feel able to visit schools, take part in school assemblies, or even teach the occasional lesson.

Chapter eight goes beyond the job of description accomplished by the earlier chapters to use sophisticated statistical procedures in order to tease out some of the relationships that exist between the amount of contact that the rural Anglican churches have with adults and young people and certain other factors. For example, I wanted to know how the number of people who come to church on a Sunday actually related to the size of the parish in which they live. In other words, I was interested in discovering whether there were specific sizes of community in which rural Anglican congregations were more viable than others. Is there generally a fixed proportion of every community interested in coming to church on a Sunday, or do church congregations tend to settle down to the same size irrespective of the pool of parishioners on which they can draw? In particular, I was curious to know whether the size of church congregations is related to the number of parishes over which the clergyman has pastoral care and the age of the clergyman himself. When clergymen look after more than one church, does the size of their congregation suffer at all? Do older clergymen tend to have more or less people present in their rural Anglican congregations?

Chapter nine examines the effect of one of the major resources still available to rural Anglicanism to influence its work among young people, namely the presence of church schools. According to the provision of the 1944 Education Act, the Church of England has still retained a considerable investment in the provision of voluntary aided and voluntary controlled schools. The majority of these schools operate at the primary rather than the secondary level and a good proportion of them are in rural situations. I wanted to know the extent to which the Anglican clergy in a rural diocese exercise their rights by way of enjoying contact with their schools. I was also curious to know whether the presence of a church school in the benefice makes any difference to the number of young people with whom the churches have contact, either on Sunday or during the week.

Chapter ten employs the data from the survey in yet another different way. The emphasis of chapters four through nine has been on abstraction, generalisation and the construction of statistical models for the purpose of analysing trends and establishing the existence of consistent patterns. However, this is only part of the story that can be told from the survey. As well as enabling us to make useful generalisations about the work going on throughout the diocese, the completed questionnaires also give us detailed insights into what is happening in the individual benefices. What chapter ten does, therefore, is to select ten of the benefices and to describe them in detail. The ten benefices have been chosen to represent a wide variety of different situations in the diocese and different types of responses to these situations. In this way, chapter ten provides windows into the unique worlds of the many benefices which have contributed to the development of our understanding of rural Anglicanism today.

Chapters three through ten demonstrate just how much insight into rural Anglicanism can be generated by the kind of survey which is conducted through a questionnaire. There are, of course, limitations to the kind of information which can be provided by the questionnaire method of research. The third of my research projects sets out to supplement what can be learnt from the questionnaire type of study by using a different research method. Instead of relying upon the answers of clergymen to questionnaires, this third project used the technique of participant observers. This means that a group of people who had been trained in the technique actually went along to attend a number of church services and to report on what they found happening there.

The research method of participant observation permits not only an accurate counting of the congregation and an estimate of the age of each attender, but also allows considerable detail to be reported about the content and presentation of the services themselves, as well as about the appearance of the church building and the attitudes of the worshippers. This technique also provides an opportunity to check the information given by the clergymen in their questionnaires. I was curious to know whether there might be a general tendency among clergy to either over-estimate or under-estimate the size of their usual church attendance.

The problem with the participant observer method of research is that it is very expensive in terms of time and commitment. This project was in fact only made possible in the first place by the volunteer labour of a group of ordinands, and there was certainly no way in which it would have been possible to cover the whole of the diocese by this method.

What I decided to do, therefore, was to select just one rural deanery, to identify all the services taking place in that deanery on one Sunday in the month, and then to arrange for each service to be attended by one participant observer.

The information gathered by this project is very rich and valuable. Chapter eleven describes in detail just what the group of ordinands found in this rural deanery. Then chapter twelve looks in depth at nine of the services attended by these visitors. Here both the strengths and the weaknesses of rural Anglicanism are exposed. To begin with, profiles are presented of two early morning Holy Communion services, one in a village of about 1,000 inhabitants and the other in a village of about 200 inhabitants. Then three mid-morning Holy Communion services are described in villages ranging from 1,200 to 2,200 inhabitants. Next, we visit two late morning services, a Matins in a village of 100 habitants and a surprise service, advertised as a Communion but in fact appearing as something quite different, in a village of nearly 200 inhabitants. Finally, we attend two Evensongs, one at 3.30 p.m. in a village of about 700 inhabitants and the other at 6.30 p.m. in the largest community in the deanery.

Finally, chapter thirteen turns the focus of this book away from the researcher, back to the local rural churches themselves and back to all of us who share a concern for the life and work of the rural Anglican church, especially as it involves young people. I have not written a chapter of summary or set out my own personal conclusions. The issues at stake are too important for such treatment. Instead, I have articulated the questions which each chapter raises in my own mind and which I believe local churches would be wise to discuss and to study.

I hope that this final chapter will become the basis through which local rural churches will be able to assess their current work among young people in particular and plan realistically for their future work. If the empirical research which I have undertaken achieves this, many of the hopes of the Diocesan Education Committee which first prompted the study will have been realised.

2 HISTORICAL PERSPECTIVE

When one is living through a period of steady but gradual change, it is often very difficult to stand back far enough from what is taking place in order really to appreciate the full extent of the changes that are happening. An analogy which I find helpful to illustrate this fact is based on the way in which the main shopping street in most towns is constantly undergoing change. When we are accustomed to walk through that street every week we are hardly conscious of the radical transformations taking place. First one shop front is rebuilt and then another whole building is demolished and replaced. Over a period of thirty years or so the whole appearance of the street may have been radically changed, but we only become aware of the extent of what has happened when we are able to place side by side photographs taken of the same street at different points in time.

My impression was that the whole face of rural Anglicanism had been steadily but gradually changing over the past thirty years, and what I wanted to be able to do was to compare photographs of rural Anglicanism taken at different points in time during the past thirty years. In this case, the researcher's photograph album needs to be tables of statistics.

The range of statistics available to the researcher is obviously limited to those which have been systematically recorded over the past thirty years. The three main sources available are the diocesan records, the diocesan year books and *The Church of England Year Book*. Although the range of statistics preserved by these sources is not wide, it is sufficient to give us valuable insights into the changes that have been taking place.

Of particular value is the information assembled by the statistical unit of the Central Board of Finance of the Church of England, and made publicly available through *The Church of England Year Book* and the Statistical Supplements. Since the mid-1950s, *The Church of England Year Book* has published fairly consistent tables of statistics charting various aspects of church membership. Generally, a fairly full set of statistics has been published biennially, although for a period in the 1970s they were published triennially. The main indices of change which it is possible to compute from *The Church of England Year Book* and the Statistical Supplements in relationship to the individual dioceses are concerned with electoral roll sizes, population figures, communicant numbers at Easter and Christmas, baptisms, confirmations and the number of diocesan clergy and readers.

Electoral roll

I began by examining the trend which had taken place in the number of people registered on the electoral rolls of the parishes in this diocese. In some senses, the electoral roll can be regarded as a list of registered church members. There are, however, problems in understanding precisely what such registration means. For example, there can be a number of reasons for individuals seeking or accepting such registration apart from seeing themselves as active church members. Some clergy may adopt a rigorous policy of only encouraging active church members to seek enrolment, while others may use the roll as a method of keeping in touch with fringe members. Of more serious significance, the general attitude towards the electoral roll may well have undergone change during the past thirty years as the attempt has been made to bring the roll into line with a more realistic estimate of active church membership. This means that we need to be extremely cautious when attempting to interpret trends revealed by the number of names on the electoral rolls of the parishes, since registration may have meant different things at different points during the past thirty years.

In 1950 the electoral rolls of the parishes stood at 52,538. Eight years later, in 1958, very little change had taken place: the electoral rolls for the parishes still stood at 52,310. During the next twelve years, there was a gradual and persistent decline, until in 1970 the electoral rolls of the parishes had fallen to 45,814.

It was in 1972 that the parishes were required by the Church Representation Rules to draw up an entirely new electoral roll, and then to prepare an entirely new roll in every succeeding sixth year. The notion behind this request was to provide for a regular pruning away of dead wood from the electoral rolls of the parishes. Inevitably, the first published returns after the 1972 preparation of the new rolls revealed a marked drop in numbers. Whereas in 1970 there were 45,814 names recorded on the electoral rolls of the parishes, in 1973 there were only 36,441. After the next preparation of a new roll the numbers fell further to 30,654 in 1978, rising again marginally to 31,200 in 1982.

Thus, during the three decades between 1950 and 1982 the number of parishioners in touch with the Anglican churches in the diocese, in the sense of having their names recorded on the electoral rolls of the parishes, had fallen by 40% from 52,538 to 31,200. This decrease in church membership has at the same time to be seen against the steady increase in the number of people actually living in the diocese. In 1951 the population stood at 390,754. By 1982 it had increased by 38% to 541,000.

Another way of measuring the change that has taken place in church membership in the diocese is to review the number of people registered on the electoral rolls as a proportion of the parishioners eligible for such registration. In 1951, the electoral rolls of the parishes carried the names of about 18.7% of the parishioners who were old enough for such registration. In 1982, the proportion had fallen to about 7.9%.

Church attendance

Given the problems involved in interpreting the electoral roll figures as a reliable index of church membership, we might be on safer ground if we were to rely on church attendance. Church attendance is probably a more accurate index of committed church contact. Unfortunately, the Church of England has kept no systematic central records of regular church attendance. The nearest approximation to this is the communicant numbers for the major Christian feasts of Easter and Christmas. In certain senses Easter and Christmas communicant figures are liable both to under-estimate and to over-estimate church attendance.

On the one hand, communicant figures tend to under-estimate church attendance by ignoring the number of church attenders who are non-communicants or who attend non-eucharistic services at the major festivals. On the other hand, festival figures over-estimate church attendance by failing to indicate the extent to which regular congregations are inflated by the casual attenders who appear only at the major Christian festivals. Nevertheless, it can be argued that these sources of error are likely to remain consistent over time, so that the comparison of Easter and Christmas communicants from different years is likely to serve as a more valuable index of religious change than the raw figures themselves serve as an accurate estimate of church membership at any given time.

The Easter and Christmas figures are available for the diocese in a consistent form from 1956 to 1982. The first thing to note is that in 1956 the festival of Easter was more popularly observed by communicants than the festival of Christmas. While Easter communicant figures, including the whole of Easter week, stood at 33,953, the Christmas figures stood at more than 7,000 less at 26,631. During the following twenty-five years, the consistent pattern has been both for the number of Easter communicants to fall and the number of Christmas communicants to rise, so that in 1980 the two figures are almost identical, with 29,000 Easter communicants and 29,200 Christmas communicants.

When Easter and Christmas communicant figures are compared for 1956 and 1982, the number of Easter communicants has dropped during this period of twenty-seven years by 14% while the number of Christmas communicants has risen by 6%. According to the former index there appears to have been a drop in church attendance, while according to the latter there seems to have been an increase. However, on closer analysis this apparent increase in Christmas communicants does not offer as much real encouragement for the rural church as it seems to do at first glance.

Another way of assessing the trends of Easter and Christmas communicants is the placing of these numbers against the steady rise in the population of the diocese throughout the past twenty-five years. The convention adopted by *The Church of England Year Book* is the calculation of the communicants as a percentage of the estimated population aged over fourteen years. Although admittedly an arbitrary age level, this statistic provides a useful index of comparison. According to this criterion, the Easter communicants in the Anglican parishes have fallen from 11% in 1956 to 6.9% in 1982 of the population aged over fourteen, while the Christmas communicants have fallen from 8.6% in 1956 to 6.6% in 1982. When viewed in this way, both the Easter and Christmas communicant figures indicate that rural Anglicanism is losing ground in relationship to the proportion of the population with whom it has established contact.

Baptism

While electoral roll and communicant numbers provide some indication of comparatively active church membership, infant baptism figures bring us directly into contact with the wider fringes of church membership. It is well known that a number of families seek baptism in the Anglican church for their young children, even though they may have little active contact with the life of the local Anglican church themselves. The Anglican clergy are far from having adopted a common mind on their attitude towards the baptism of infants from non-practising families. While some argue that such indiscriminate baptism, as they may wish to style it, makes nonsense of the theology of baptism and the promises entailed in it, others argue that they would rather encourage nominal Anglicanism than a total disregard for what the Anglican churches stand for. I was interested to observe the trend that has taken place in infant baptism in the diocese during the past twenty-five years.

In 1956 there were 4,079 infant baptisms at the Anglican fonts in the diocese. This figure remained roughly stable until 1970, when 3,924 infant baptisms took place. Meanwhile, the number of live births being registered in the area covered by the diocese rose from 6,455 in 1956 to 7,730 in 1970. Thus, while in 1956 63.2% of the children born in the diocese were baptised as infants at Anglican fonts, the proportion had fallen to 50.8% in 1970. Throughout the 1970s the proportion of the live births baptised as infants continued to fall steadily to 47.5% in 1973, 42.4% in 1976, 39.6% in 1978, 38.8% in 1980 and 36.6% in 1982. Currently less than two-fifths of the children born in the diocese are being brought to the Anglican church as infants for baptism. This decline in infant baptism may well be a very significant prediction for the strength of rural Anglicanism in the future, as more and more young people grow up without even feeling the nominal adherence to the Anglican church conferred on the previous generation by infant baptism.

Alongside the decline in infant baptism, there has been a small increase in the number of other baptisms taking place, although this figure has never been very large. In 1956 there were 270 more mature baptisms. Then for each year in which figures are available between 1958 and 1976 there were between 120 and 220 more mature baptisms. In 1978 the figure rose to 596 and again in 1980 to 610 and in 1982 to 640. The sharp rise between 1976 and 1978 is largely to be accounted by by the fact that the 1978 returns defined for the first time infant baptisms as those under one year of age. Thus an eighteen month old child would have been clasified among the infants in 1976, but among the adults in the 'other persons' category in 1978. At the same time it is likely that some of these other persons include unbaptised teenagers and adults who wish to be confirmed in the Anglican church. Obviously as the practice of infant baptism declines, the option of adult believer's baptism is more readily available for those who turn to the church later in life.

Confirmation

While the infants who are baptised can, at the best, only be seen as passive members of the Anglican church, the teenagers and adults who present themselves for confirmation can be seen as expressing a more active and personal commitment to Anglicanism. Indeed, confirmation figures provide interesting insights into the recruitment pattern of rural Anglicanism. Throughout the eight year period between 1955 and 1962, confirmations ran at an average of 2,824 per year in the diocese. Then, during the next eleven year period there was a persistent decline, falling to 2,444 in 1963, 1,915 in 1965, 1,650 in 1967, 1,332 in 1970, 1,089 in 1972 and the all time low of 684 in 1973. Throughout the rest of the 1970s the confirmation figures varied between 1,096 and 1,232. The number of people confirmed in this rural Anglican diocese in either 1982 or 1983 represents only one-third of those confirmed in 1955. The pool of confirmed members upon whom the rural Anglican church can draw is thus rapidly declining.

One other interesting fact emerges from the inspection of the confirmation figures over the past twenty-five years. In the 1950s and early 1960s, more males were presenting themselves for confirmation than females. In rural Anglicanism confirmation was still being seen as an accepted rite of passage for the adolescent male. In 1967 this ratio changed so that more females were presenting themselves for confirmation than males, and this has remained the consistent case through to 1983. This is an important indication of the decreasing impact that the rural Anglican church is making among men and youths.

Clergy

Alongside this steady decline in membership, church attendance, infant baptism and confirmation, rural Anglican dioceses have been busy reducing their stipendiary full-time clerical manpower in line with the recommendations of the *Sheffield Report* on the deployment of the clergy. A useful piece of information published in *The Church of England Year Book* concerns the total number of full-time stipendiary clergy employed in each diocese. The clerical manpower of the rural Anglican diocese under review remained basically constant between 1957 and 1969. In 1957 there were 286 full-time diocesan clergy and in 1969 there were 292. Since the population of the diocese was rising during this period, the steady state of the clerical manpower implied a slight widening in the clergy-population ratio. While in 1957 there was one full-time diocesan clergyman for every 1,417 individuals living in the diocese, the ratio had widened in 1969 to one full-time diocesan clergyman for every 1,630 residents.

It was during the 1970s that the radical running down of clerical manpower began. Whereas in 1969 there were 292 full-time diocesan clergy in the diocese, in 1979 there were only 204, a reduction of 30% in only a decade. Since 1979 the total number of full-time diocesan clergy in the diocese has risen slightly to 212 in 1983. This slight increase means that at December 1983 the diocese was employing 26 clergymen in excess of its Sheffield allocation and so is required still to reduce its clerical manpower considerably further. The significance of the reduction that has already taken place is again usefully illustrated by reference to the clergy-population ratio. By 1982 the ratio had widened to one full-time diocesan clergyman for every 2,613 residents. Had the Sheffield targets for 1982 been reached, the ratio would have stood at one full-time diocesan clergyman for every 2,924 residents. Another obvious consequence of the running down of the clerical manpower is an increase in the number of churches being cared for by an individual priest.

One of the ways in which rural Anglicanism is attempting to compensate for the loss of clerical manpower is through the expansion of lay ministry. Increasingly lay ministers are being required in order to keep the services of the rural churches going. The office of reader is now a well established ministry in the Church of England, involving authorisation to lead the services of Matins and Evensong, to assist at Communion, to preach and to undertake pastoral responsibilities. During the past twenty-five years there has been a steady increase in the number of readers licensed to officiate in the diocese. In 1956 there were 117 licensed readers. By 1966 this number had risen to 149. During the next ten years it had risen further to 173 in 1976. By 1983 there were 204 readers licensed in the diocese.

At the same time this diocese has pioneered a second type of lay ministry in the form of elders, a notion formally approved by the Diocesan Conference in 1968. Elders are licensed to undertake various forms of pastoral ministry, to assist at Communion and to read the offices, although they are not permitted to preach. Significantly, no formal training is required before admission to the office of elder. Unfortunately no systematic record has been kept of the growth in this form of lay ministry. By 1980 there were about 120 elders licensed in the diocese. By 1984 the number had risen to 167.

The expansion of lay ministry has, theoretically, given some form of equality of opportunity for women to share in the ministry of the rural Anglican church. In theory women have as much opportunity to undertake the lay ministry of reader and elder as men. In practice, however, both of these lay ministries have tended to remain male dominated. According to the 1983 figures, just 27 of the 204 licenced readers in the diocese were women. In other words there are nearly seven male readers for every one female reader. According to the 1984 figures, 56 of the 167 elders licenced in the diocese were women. In other words there are twice as many male elders as female elders. It is also interesting to note that in 1982 the total ministry of the diocese involved just 1 stipendiary and 2 non-stipendiary deaconesses.

Schools

One further index of the changes talking place in rural Anglicanism is provided by an analysis of the statistics regarding church voluntary aided and controlled schools. School figures accounting for both county and voluntary schools in a diocese are difficult to come by. I was extremely grateful to the local education authority for compiling for me figures for the county which is almost although not exactly co-terminus with the geographical area covered by the diocese. The local education authority was able to assemble these figures for me for the period 1967 to 1980 inclusive. It has not proved to be possible to draw back the veil before 1967.

In 1967 there were 117 Church of England voluntary controlled schools in the county. By 1980, 21 of these schools had been closed, leaving a total of 96. In 1967 there were 31 Church of England voluntary aided schools in the county. By 1980, 11 of these had been closed, leaving a total of 20. Thus, during the fourteen year period the stock of voluntary controlled schools had been reduced by 18% and the stock of voluntary aided schools had been reduced by 35%. Under the provision of the 1944 Education Act, it is through the voluntary aided status that the denomination responsible for the foundation of the school retains the greater control. The fall in the number of Anglican schools during this period can be accounted for in terms of the closure of small and elderly rural schools. This process was accelerated in the early 1970s when part of the county reorganised its educational system into the three tier structure of first, middle and upper schools, thus reducing the number of pupils attending the neighbourhood primary schools and leading to the closure of the smaller village schools.

Another way of assessing the changing role of Anglican voluntary schools is by calculating the proportion of the total number of full-time pupils in maintained primary and secondary schools in the county who are in fact attending Anglican schools. In 1980, 10.4% of the children at school in the county were attending Church of England voluntary controlled schools, compared with 11.6% in 1967. In 1980, 3.3% of the children at school in the county were attending Church of England voluntary aided schools, compared with 6.0% in 1967. Overall, the Anglican stake in the county has dropped during this period of fourteen years from 17.6% to 13.7% of the occupied school places. The opportunities which rural Anglicanism formerly enjoyed to influence young people through their secular schooling are being slowly eroded.

It has not been my intention in this chapter to debate the cases for and against such issues as the place of church schools in a rural diocese or the implementation of the Sheffield recommendations on the deployment of clergy. My aim has been simply to draw attention to the statistical trends in the conviction that such information provides the essential data from which any evaluation of the current state of rural Anglicanism must proceed.

3 THE SURVEY

The information derived from existing statistics and discussed in the previous chapter begins to paint a picture of rural Anglicanism today, but it does so in very broad brush strokes and with relatively crude lines. The present survey was organised in order to provide much more detail and accuracy to the picture. Different aspects of the results of this new survey are discussed carefully in chapters four through ten. However, before turning to the results of the survey, it is necessary to focus attention on the survey itself. What did the survey set out to achieve, and why? What kind of questionnaire was used? How was the questionnaire distributed throughout the diocese? How many clergymen completed it and how many threw it away? How representative and how reliable are the results? And what kind of diocese is it anyway? I will try to answer these questions in turn.

Aim

The aim of the questionnaire was to discover information about the level of contact which the churches were having in this one rural Anglican diocese with their parishioners. In particular I was concerned to learn as much as possible about the churches' contact with young people under the age of twenty-two. It seemed to me that the churches' contact with children and young people was a particular test both of the present strength of rural Anglicanism and of its prospects for the future. With this in mind, a questionnaire was drawn up in three parts, to look at Sunday services and weekday meetings, the clergyman's contact with young people, and the churches' specific provisions for young people.

The designing of questionnaires and the collecting of statistical data is a sensitive business. There was a lot of other information which I would have liked to have been able to collect from the clergymen in the diocese at the same time as they completed this short questionnaire. It would have been helpful to learn about their attitudes towards their work, about their hopes, frustrations and difficulties. However, after much thought and discussion, I decided that it would be wiser to aim solely to collect factual information and to design the questionnaire to be as simple and straightforward as possible. There were two reasons for limiting the project in this way.

First, it is one of the facts of social research that a short and simple questionnaire attracts greater co-operation and a higher response rate. I decided that it was more valuable to collect a high quality of information over a limited area, rather than to spread my net more broadly and to be less confident in the quality of the catch.

Second, again in order to assure the greatest possible level of co-operation among the clergy of the diocese, I needed the formal backing of the diocese itself. In the event, the Diocesan Education Committee not only backed the project, but also provided enthusiasm and volunteer labour that made the physical task of data collection possible. Such help was bought only at a price. The clergymen on the Diocesan Education Committee argued very strongly that probing questions about the attitudes of the Anglican clergy to their work in a rural diocese would pose an unacceptable threat to their clerical brethren. On this basis, the Diocesan Education Committee vetoed the possibility of the inclusion of such items. In the last analysis, the researcher must be content to work within the confines of the information that is available to him.

Designing the questionnaire

The questionnaire was designed to be printed on four pages, the first of which was a front cover explaining the nature and origin of the project. The second page asked the clergymen to list all the Sunday services taken in their parishes on the previous Sunday, including the services which they took themselves and which other clergymen or lay people may have taken on their behalf. They were asked to specify the time, place and type of service in each case. In this way, we could draw up a list of all the Sunday services which were happening in a rural Anglican diocese on a typical Sunday.

Alongside the listing of the Sunday services, the clergymen were asked to estimate the number of people present and to break down their congregations into a set of specified age categories. Since my primary interest was in understanding the churches' contact with children and young people aged twenty-two and under, the following age categories were used in order to group the children and young people into convenient four year age bands. The age bands selected were two to five year olds, six to nine year olds, ten to thirteen year olds, fourteen to seventeen year olds, eighteen to twenty-one year olds, and adults over the age of twenty-one. In this way we could draw up a detailed profile of the age structure of those attending services in a rural Anglican diocese.

It is appreciated that the assignment of church congregations to such age bands may be arbitrary and that some error and guess-work may be involved. The results of the survey need to be read in the light of this word of caution. However, there are two good reasons for still pursuing the study in spite of this acknowledged difficulty. First, it is unlikely that a more reliable method could be found to suggest answers to the same kind of questions, apart from the much lengthier process of inviting each church attender to complete a questionnaire for himself or herself. Until the resources can be made available to make such an ambitious project possible, the present survey method provides the best interim estimate of church attenders that we can construct. Second, the guesswork and errors are themselves of considerable interest because they give us a direct indication of the clergymen's perceptions of the age structure of their congregations, as well as of the total number of people who come to their services.

After looking at the pattern of Sunday services, page two of the questionnaire asks the clergymen to list the other forms of meetings that took place in their parishes on the previous Sunday in addition to services. Again, they were asked to indicate the number of people in each age band who attended. Finally, this part of the questionnaire asked the clergymen to list all the weekday activities which had taken place in their benefice during the past week and to which some children or young people had come. Again, they were asked to indicate the number of people in each age band who attended. In this way, we were able to assemble a complete description of the total contact between the churches of a rural Anglican diocese and young people during the course of a typical week.

Information from page two of the questionnaire was coded for computer analysis in two ways. First, the benefices were taken as the unit of study. For each benefice, three sets of figures were abstracted from the replies to the questionnaire for computer input. These were the total Sunday contact for each age band, the total weekday contact for each age band, and the aggregated Sunday and weekday contact for each age band. Second, the individual services were taken as the unit of study. For each service, information about the time and type of service was abstracted, together with the number of people present within each of the age bands.

As well as asking the clergymen to give details of what had happened in their parishes during the previous week, page two of the questionnaire also asked them to select and to describe some of their regular or irregular 'special services'. This gave them the opportunity to mention the kind of services which had not happened on the previous Sunday, but which, happening from time to time, attracted an extra number of children and young people. Since the aim of this question was to give us an insight into rural Anglicanism when it is flourishing at its best, each clergyman was encouraged to select the most promising occasions from the recent past. The replies to this question were not of the kind which it would have made sense to load on to the computer, since they contained such a diversity of information. Instead, they provide some very valuable illustrations of what is happening in different parishes from time to time and these illustrations are fully discussed in the later chapters.

Page three of the questionnaire sets out to gather a different kind of information. It turns attention away from attendance at services and meetings to look specifically at the points of contact between the churches and young people in this rural Anglican diocese. This part of the questionnaire lists twenty-four specific potential meeting points between the young and the church. In relationship to each of these twenty-four meeting points, the clergymen were asked to rate the level of actual contact on a four point scale ranging from 'at least once a week' through 'often' and 'occasionally' to 'never'. The response 'not appropriate' was also provided as an alternative response to 'never'.

The twenty-four potential meeting points listed in this part of the questionnaire included six questions about whether brownies, cubs, guides, scouts, boys/girls brigade or other uniformed organisations come to church. A further four questions asked whether the clergyman visits local brownies, cubs, guides or scouts. Nine questions explored the clergyman's contact with schools, asking whether he leads assemblies, takes lessons or makes informal visits in local primary or first schools, middle schools, or secondary or upper schools. Questions were also asked in this section about whether other denominations work with young people in the benefice, whether the clergyman co-operates with other denominations in youth work, whether the clergyman has contact with any Local Education Authority youth groups, and whether any members of the local church congregation work in youth clubs and so create an informal link in this way between the church and young people.

Page four of the questionnaire examined the actual provisions made by the churches themselves, either specifically for children and young people or for adults but which also attract children and young people aged between two and twenty-one years of age. Sixteen types of provision were listed in this part of the questionnaire. These were Sunday schools, youth clubs mainly for church members, youth clubs mainly for non-church members, church lads/church girls'/boys' brigade, pathfinders, CYFA, church sponsored cubs, scouts and venture scouts, church sponsored brownies, guides and ranger guides, current confirmation classes, those confirmed during the previous year, house groups, bell ringers, choir at service, choir at regular practice, servers, parochial church council members. Again the clergymen were asked to specify the number of individuals within each age band who were involved in each of these sixteen provisions. The age bands used in this part of the questionnaire were the same as those specified in the first section of the questionnaire. The replies to this final part of the questionnaire enable us to complete our detailed profile of the churches' contact with children and young people in a rural Anglican diocese.

In addition to the information made available from the questionnaire, the computer input included population figures and electoral roll figures, both for parishes and for benefices, abstracted from the *1978 Diocesan Year Book*, and the clergymen's ages culled from the diocesan records and *Crockford's Clerical Directory*.

Distributing the questionnaire

Once the questionnaire had been tried out on a few clergymen in a neighbouring diocese, the survey was ready to begin. The sampling strategy was planned in co-operation with the Diocesan Education Committee. The intention was to collect information from every parish in the diocese by distributing the questionnaire to every clergyman in charge of a parish or set of parishes. The first step was to draw up a complete list of the clergymen to be contacted, and this was done on the basis of the information contained in the most recent *Diocesan Year Book*.

The list named 185 clergymen who had been indentified by the *Diocesan Year Book* as being in charge of a parish or group of parishes, and who were still in charge at the time when the survey was carried out. Throughout the following discussion, these 185 units in the care of individual clergymen are described as benefices, although strictly speaking some of the clergymen were in charge of churches from more than one legally constituted benefice, and a few legally constituted benefices were, for one reason or another, distributed among the care of more than one clergyman. The term benefice is, thus, used consistently and solely to describe the parishes in the actual care of one clergyman.

At the time when the survey was carried out, in addition to the 185 clergymen indentified, there were also 21 benefices which were either vacant when the *Diocesan Year Book* had been compiled or had subsequently fallen vacant. Although some of these benefices had been recently filled, it seemed that these clergymen were so recently appointed to their parishes that they ought not to be included in the study. Thus, all of these 21 benefices were excluded from the sample. In addition to this there were a further 10 individual parishes, as distinct from benefices, which were either looked after by retired clergymen, whose addresses were not included in the *Diocesan Year Book*'s list of clergy, or which had somehow been temporarily 'lost' in pastoral reorganisation and which had not been picked up through the information available in the *Diocesan Year Book*.

The list of 185 clergymen in charge of a parish or group of parishes provided the names and addresses of those to whom the questionnaire was to be distributed. The next problem was to decide how most effectively to distribute the questionnaire. Experience suggests that the best response to questionnaires comes when time is taken actually to go and talk with the people whose co-operation and help is needed. This kind of personal contact allows the reasons for doing the research to be fully explained and any hestitations about matters like the value and confidentiality of the replies to be openly and frankly discussed.

One hundred and eighty-five personal visits seems a daunting prospect, especially given the need to telephone and to arrange mutually convenient times for each visit. It was here that the help of lay members of the Diocesan Education Committee, together with a few other lay people from the deaneries, proved to be invaluable. The diocese was divided into areas, roughly consistent with the rural deaneries, and the team of lay helpers took responsibility for one area each. In this way, all of the 185 clergymen were personally visited over a relatively short space of time. The questionnaire was left for them to complete in their own time and the visitor arranged to call back to collect it. After a reasonable space of time had elapsed, I personally telephoned or arranged to visit the clergymen who had not returned their questionnaires. I learnt a lot from this experience. Eventually, only 14 of the 185 clergymen approached refused to help with the project or failed to return a completed questionnaire. This means that there was a response rate of 92.4%. Such a remarkably high response rate is due largely to the care and patience of those who helped with the personal distribution of the questionnaires.

When the 171 completed questionnaires had been returned, it was possible to assess how representative these were of the whole diocese. In the whole diocese there were 206 benefice units. Twenty-one of these were not included in the study and 14 refused to co-operate. The completed questionnaires thus represent 83% of the total number of benefices in the diocese. The 171 benefices from which information was available contained 403 separate parishes. In the whole diocese there are 493 parishes. The completed questionnaires thus represent 81.7% of the total number of parishes in the diocese. The completed questionnaires also represent 84.5% of the total number of parishioners on the electoral rolls of the parishes and 92% of the total population of the diocese. On all of these criteria, the survey results seem to cover a highly satisfactory proportion of the diocese.

There is however, just one marked difference between the clergymen who completed the questionnaire and those who refused to do so. The average age of those who refused or failed to take part in the survey is almost ten years higher than that of those who co-operated in the research. The average age of the clergymen who co-operated in the project is 52.6 years, while the average age of the clergymen who failed to complete the questionnaire was 61.2 years. This seems to indicate a greater unwillingness among the older clergymen to co-operate in this kind of research study. This greater unwillingness possibly results from a greater antipathy towards survey methods and statistical research, or a greater sense of anxiety or threat among the older clergymen when they are asked to reveal the scope of their contact with adult and young parishioners for scrutiny by someone else.

Before turning to the information made available from the completed questionnaires, it will be helpful to try to get to know in greater detail the nature of the benefices which have supplied the information. What kind of rural Anglican diocese are we dealing with? What sort of size are these benefices? How many people live in them? How many names are on the electoral rolls? How many of the benefices contain more than one parish? How old are the clergymen who minister in these benefices? To what extent are the clergy in charge of these benefices supported by team ministries, by stipendiary curates and by those ordained to non-stipendiary pastoral ministry?

Population

All told the population of these 171 benefices totals just over 500,000 parishioners. This means that the average population for each benefice is just under 3,000. This average, however, conceals a very wide difference between the smallest benefices and the largest. On the one hand, there are 12 benefices in the diocese which do not muster as many as 500 parishioners each. Two of these are inner-city benefices in depopulated zones in the largest town in the diocese. The other 10 are small rural benefices. A further 50 of the 171 benefices have between 500 and 1,000 inhabitants each; 33 of the benefices have between 1,000 and 1,500 people living in each of them, and another 17 have between 1,500 and 2,000 each. This means that two-thirds (66%) of the clergymen with whom we are dealing have less than 2,000 inhabitants in their pastoral care and one-third (36%) of them have less than 1,000. At the other extreme, there are 13 benefices in the sample which have over 10,000 parishioners, with the largest suburban parish boasting 25,000 inhabitants.

In terms of the total population of their benefices, the rural clergy may appear to have an easy time in comparison with their urban colleagues. However, if population figures are taken as the primary index of the clergymen's workload, it is necessary to be clear about his anticipated relationship with that population. In the rural situation of a benefice of under 2,000 inhabitants it may well still be possible for the parish priest to establish his own identity in the community and to build up relationships with the inhabitants outside the immediate sphere of the active church membership. Historically, this has been one of the strengths of rural Anglicanism and possibly a major reason for the Anglican church's ability to retain the support of a much higher proportion of rural populations than it has been able to do in urban or suburban situations. The withdrawal of the clergy from the countryside on the grounds of establishing a fairer priest-population ratio throughout urban and rural areas may have the consequence not only of helping the urban areas but also of extending the failure of urban Anglicanism into the countryside as well.

An analysis of the number of people living in each benefice is a useful indication of the total size of the community being cared for by each clergyman. These figures do not, however, accurately reflect the actual size of the communities in the individual parishes, since many of the benefices are multi-parish units. There are in fact 403 separate parishes within the 171 benefices. The population of these 403 parishes range in size from a tiny rural hamlet which has just 13 adults living in it to the largest parish in the diocese, the single parish benefice of 25,000 inhabitants already mentioned above. Almost two-thirds (65%) of the parishes are very small communities of less than 500 inhabitants and three-quarters (77.4%) have no more than 1,000 inhabitants. Almost all of these small parishes are in rural areas, apart from the one or two parishes in de-populated zones in the largest town in the diocese. In the majority of cases, each of these small rural communities is responsible for the maintenance of a medieval church. At the other extreme, less than one in eleven of the parishes (8.6%) has more than 5,000 inhabitants, and only 3.2% are bigger than 10,000 inhabitants.

Electoral roll

While the population figures give an idea of the number of residents within the pastoral care of each clergyman in the diocese, the electoral roll figures for the benefices provide some indication of the number of committed Anglicans among whom he is exercising his ministry. Nine of the 171 benefices have less than 50 names on their electoral rolls, while a further 41 have between 51 and 100 names. This means that nearly one-third (30%) of the clergymen are dealing with a church membership of less than 100 adults. Fifty-two benefices have between 101 and 150 names on their electoral rolls, while a further 28 have between 151 and 200 names. Looked at in this way, three-quarters of the clergymen in the diocese are ministering to church memberships of less than 200 adults. At the other end of the scale, just 10% of the benefices have a membership in excess of 300. The largest recorded electoral roll figure for a benefice in the diocese is 452 names.

Once again, when looking at the electoral rolls, it is helpful to turn attention not only to the benefice but to the individual parishes as well. At the parish level, the electoral roll figures give a good indication of the number of committed people upon whom each church can draw, not only to support the liturgy and to bear the running costs, but also to maintain the medieval fabric. The smallest electoral roll contains only 7 names. One quarter (26%) of the parish churches have no more than 25 names on their electoral roll, while three out of every five (58%) of the parish churches have no more than 50 names on their roll. At the other end of the scale, only one in six of the churches (16%) has more than 100 names on the electoral roll.

These electoral roll figures begin to draw attention to the precarious nature of some of the rural Anglican churches, especially when it is appreciated that electoral roll figures tend to inflate the actual size of active church membership. The rural clergy often have very small Christian communities on which to draw and among whom to share the work associated with the maintenance and extension of the Christian church in their benefices. Rural communities can no longer necessarily be seen as strongholds of Anglicanism. The work required in the villages of the clergy is in no sense simply that of maintaining Christian communities, but the much more difficult task of proclaiming the gospel in a secular society and of building up new Christian fellowships.

Parishes

The reduction in clerical manpower and the amalgamation of parishes means that it is becoming more and more rare for a clergyman working in a rural Anglican diocese to have only one church in his care. Thus, three out of every five of the benefices in the sample (62%) now have 2 or more parishes in them, while well over a third (37%) have 3 or more parishes. The largest number of parishes in any one benefice in the sample is 7, and there are 2 benefices of this size among the 171 respondents to the questionnaire.

The amalgamation of parishes in this way has implications both for the rural Anglican churches and for the Anglican clergymen. As far as the churches are concerned, it means that 232 of the 403 parishes are now being run without a resident clergyman: the Anglican clergyman is no longer part of the residential life of these communities. When considerable distances, as well as travelling expenses, are involved between the parishes, the priest's casual visiting of his parishioners and even his contact with the church building may tend to become concentrated in the parish in which he lives. At the same time, it becomes more difficult for the parishioners who live in the other parishes to casually visit the vicarage and to draw upon the resources of the local clergyman. As far as the clergymen are concerned, 106 of the 171 men are now responsible for conducting worship in more than one church, chairing more than one parochial church council, working with more than one set of churchwardens, organists and so on, relating to the life of more than one distinct community, and accepting some responsibility for the maintenance and upkeep of more than one church building. For 28 of these men, their responsibility extends to 4 or more distinct units. On Sundays, these clergymen find themselves with a major problem in trying to move between a series of different churches. Consequently, services can become rushed and inadequately prepared.

Clergy

While the workload of the clergy in a rural Anglican diocese is increasing, their average age is still relatively high. With the amalgamation of parishes the rural ministry is ceasing to maintain the idyllic retirement image. The average age of the clergymen in charge of the 171 benefices was 52.6 years. Nearly three in ten of the benefices (28%) are served by clergymen aged over sixty. In fact, the oldest clergymen in charge of a benefice responding to the questionnaire was aged seventy-seven, while the eighty-seven year old clergyman in charge of another benefice in the diocese declined to take part in the survey. Another three in ten of the benefices (30%) are served by clergymen aged between fifty-one and sixty. This means that only four in ten of the benefices in this rural Anglican diocese are served by clergymen aged under fifty-one. At the younger end of the age range, the 171 benefices include 8 clergymen aged thirty-five and under, 15 aged between thirty-six and forty, 22 aged between forty-one and forty-five and 21 aged between forty-six and fifty.

The changing nature of rural ministry, as a consequence both of expecting rural clergy to look after more parishes and also of the diminishing commitment to Christianity among those who live in the villages, is placing a new set of strains on the clergy, an increasing workload and new demands for flexibility and mobility. The image of rural ministry is changing, and it may increasingly require the energy and skills of younger clergy to meet the contemporary demands.

Historically, the Anglican church has been organised in such a way that clergymen tend to be working on their own in their own benefice without any formal form of shared professional ministry. This has been particularly the case in smaller rural benefices where resources have not been available for the appointment of curates. In the case of the 171 benefices responding to the survey, only 9 of them were able to support a curate, and these 9 were all in urban contexts within a predominantly rural diocese.

In recent years, two other forms of shared ordained ministry have been developed which help to break down the professional isolation of the rural clergymen. These are team ministries and the deployment of men ordained to the non-stipendiary pastoral ministry. The idea of a team ministry is that a group of benefices are amalgamated and run as a single unit. A team rector is appointed as having legal responsibility for all the parishes within the larger benefice, while team vicars are appointed to assist him. Just 3 of the 171 benefices in the diocese have been organised in this way. One of these is a very small team of two, the team rector and one team vicar, while the other two are teams of just three, the team rector and two team vicars. The idea of non-stipendiary pastoral ministry involves the pastoral deployment of ordained men who are earning their living from a secular job. Just 6 of the 171 benefices seemed to enjoy the additional services of a non-stipendiary minister, although information about the non-stipendiary ministry was not too clearly organised in the diocese at the time of the survey. As far as could be gleaned from the *Diocesan Year Book*, there were no benefices where more than one type of shared ordained ministry existed, for example a curate and a non-stipendiary minister in the same benefice.

This analysis indicates that the large majority of the benefices, nine out of every ten, are served by individual clergymen who are working outside the context of any formal form of shared ordained ministry. Although the historical development of the benefice structure of the Anglican church has encouraged the notion of independence and autonomy among the clergy, the question now certainly needs to be continually raised as to whether the changing demands of rural ministry could properly benefit from a greater development of shared ministry. In an age of increasing secular professional specialisation, it may no longer be appropriate to expect the individual clergyman working in a rural benefice to possess all the skills required within the churches over which he has been given pastoral charge. The independent operation of small benefices may also involve the unnecessary duplication of some pastoral work, like the running of confirmation classes and adult training sessions. At the same time, team co-operation may enable the individual clergyman to share responsibilities and to draw on others for professional and personal support, as well as sharpening the awareness of accountability. Rural Anglicanism has still a long way to go before such notions of shared ordained ministry will become anything other than the unusual exception.

4 A HEAD COUNT

After the information supplied by the clergymen had been fed into the computer, the really interesting job of piecing together a picture of rural Anglicanism today could begin. The obvious point from which to start was to make an overall head count of the number of people with whom the churches in this rural Anglican diocese were making contact during the course of a typical week. Subsequent chapters will look in detail at the parts played by different provisions, like church services, Sunday schools and so on: this initial chapter will provide the essential background of charting the overall impact of rural Anglicanism, against which the relative contributions of different aspects of church life can be assessed.

The one distinction which this chapter needs to make in carrying out its job of head counting is between the people who have contact with the churches on a Sunday and those who have contact during the rest of the week. This is a very important distinction in the context of rural Anglicanism, since it will quickly become apparent as this chapter unfolds that there is a considerable difference between the level of Sunday activity and the level of weekday activity in the churches in the diocese.

Sunday contact

First, we shall look at the number of people with whom the churches of the 171 benefices have contact on a typical Sunday. All told these benefices have contact with 7,411 children and young people under the age of twenty-two and with 14,321 adults over the age of twenty-one. These figures include the contacts made through all Sunday meeting points, including church services, Sunday schools, youth clubs and house meetings. Two ways of assessing the meaning of the number of people with whom rural Anglicanism has contact on a Sunday is to average them across the benefices and to view them as a proportion of the total population of the parishes. According to the first of these indices, each benefice is making contact with an average of 127 children, young people and adults. According to the second of these indices, the rural Anglican churches are meeting 4.2% of their parishioners on a typical Sunday. These figures over-estimate rather than under-estimate the proportion of the population reached by the churches, since they do not take into account the occasions when the same individual has more than one contact with the church during the course of the same Sunday.

Thus, on a typical Sunday the Anglican church has contact with only about 4% of the people living in a rural diocese. On the criterion of Sunday contact with the churches, only 4 people in every 100 can be regarded as active Anglicans, while the other 96 in every 100 are outside the Anglican church. It needs to be remembered, too, that the majority of these people who are not attending the Anglican church on a Sunday are not attending other churches either. While it is very difficult to find accurate comparative data for the various denominations in a rural area, the report, *Prospect for the Eighties*, gives an important clue when it suggests that in this particular rural diocese at least 88 people in every 100 will have no contact with a church of any kind on a typical Sunday.

The fact that only 4 people in every 100 can be regarded as active Anglicans, even in a rural diocese, is an essential statistic for the rural Anglican church to grasp in order to assess its own self understanding. For many generations the Church of England was able to regard itself as a national church and as a majority movement, representing a majority culture, especially in rural society. Plainly this assumption no longer holds. It is now necessary for rural Anglicanism to see itself as a minority movement, and a very small minority movement at that, regularly touching only 4% of the population living in a rural diocese. What is now necessary for rural Anglicanism is that it should attempt to adapt itself to expressing the life of a minority community, rather than that of a majority community. Minority movements need to work hard to preserve and to propagate their distinctive identity within an alien host culture.

So much, then, for an overall view of Sunday contact. What more can we learn from looking at the number of children and young people contacted within each age band? It is plain that the rural Anglican churches have more success with some age groups than others. The two age groups most successfully contacted by rural Anglicanism on a typical Sunday are the six to nine year olds and the ten to thirteen year olds. The 171 benefices contacted 2,149 six to nine year olds and almost an equal number (2,131) of ten to thirteen year olds. The rural Anglican church has considerably less contact with children and young people in the age bands either side of the six to thirteen year olds. Thus, the 171 benefices contacted 1,028 two to five year olds, 1,355 fourteen to sixteen year olds and 748 eighteen to twenty-one year olds.

A good way of grasping the meaning of these figures is to average the number of children and young people contacted in each age band across the benefices. Such a calculation naturally conceals the great variation which exists among the benefices, but this will be examined in detail later. On average, each benefice would have contact with 12 six to nine year olds and 12 ten to thirteen year olds, compared with 6 two to five year olds, 8 fourteen to seventeen year olds and only 4 eighteen to twenty-one year olds.

When we compare the level of contact with each age group, it becomes apparent that the number of fourteen to seventeen year olds in contact with the rural Anglican church on a Sunday represents only two-thirds of the number of six to thirteen year olds, while the number of eighteen to twenty-one year olds represents only one-third of the six to thirteen year olds reached by the benefices. This suggests that, while the churches are able to recruit young people after the age of five and maintain contact with them over the next few years, a third of these young people have lost contact with the churches before they reach the next age group of fourteen to seventeen year olds, and by the time they reach the eighteen to twenty-one age band, two-thirds have lost contact with the church. Thus, these statistics highlight the extent to which the rural Anglican churches are unable to maintain the limited contact which they are successful in creating with the under fourteen year olds through adolescence into young adulthood.

Weekday contact

If the performance of rural Anglicanism in making contact with children and young people on a typical Sunday does not seem over successful, the situation during the rest of the week is considerably bleaker. The 171 benefices make contact during a typical week with 2,477 children and young people under the age of twenty-one. This is an average of 14 children and young people per benefice. The age group with which the churches make most contact during the week are the ten to thirteen year olds.

There is practically no weekday provision in rural Anglicanism for pre-schoolers. The 171 benefices contact just 117 two to five year olds during a typical week. Among the six to nine year olds, the number rises to 720, and again among the ten to thirteen year olds to exactly 1,000. There is a sharp fall off among the fourteen to seventeen year olds to

516, and a further sharp fall off among the eighteen to twenty-one year olds to just 124 individuals. Viewed from another perspective, each benefice is contacting during a typical week less than 1 two to five year old, 4 six to nine year olds, 6 ten to thirteen year olds, 3 fourteen to seventeen year olds and less than 1 eighteen to twenty-one year old.

Differences between benefices

So far we have examined the total number of children and young people in different age bands contacted by the 171 benefices. The next question is to discover the proportion of the benefices that have contact with children and young people of different ages. Do all the benefices have some contact with children and young people or are there some places which have completely lost contact with the young generation? In attempting to answer this question, it is again helpful to distinguish between Sunday and weekday activity.

The first significant fact to emerge from this type of analysis is that 12 of the 171 benefices have no contact at all with any children or young people between the ages of two and twenty-one during a typical week. In these benefices, not all of which by any means small, the rural Anglican church is making no impact whatsover on the local young community. While 12 of the benefices have no contact with any young people at all on a Sunday, 113 of them have no contact at all with any children or young people during the rest of the week. Put another way, 7% of the benefices have no contact with children or young people at all, and a further 59% have no contact with children or young people apart from on a Sunday. This leaves only one-third (34%) of the benefices which do any work with children or young people on weekdays.

On a typical Sunday, more benefices are able to make contact with six to thirteen year olds than with any other age group. Eighty-five per cent of the benefices have some Sunday contact with six to nine year olds and 84% of them have some Sunday contact with ten to thirteen year olds. The proportion of the benefices that have some Sunday contact with fourteen to seventeen year olds falls to 75%, and the proportion that have some Sunday contact with eighteen to twenty-one year olds falls even further to 61%. At the other end of the age range, 72% of the benefices have some Sunday contact with two to five year olds. These figures mean that one in four of the benefices have no Sunday contact with any fourteen to seventeen year olds, while two in five of the benefices have no Sunday contact with any eighteen to twenty-one year olds.

Many of the benefices that do have some Sunday contact with children and young people are not able to maintain this contact right through the age range. Only two in five of the benefices are able to have Sunday contact with at least one young person from each of the five age bands employed in the study. In other words, considerably less than half of the benefices are reaching the whole age range of children and young people in their care. They are leaving many age bands of children and young people completely untouched and uncatered for.

On weekdays, more benefices are able to establish contact with ten to thirteen year olds than with any other age group, but even then only 30% of the benefices are doing any work with this age group in the course of a typical week. By way of comparison, 20% of the benefices have weekday contact with six to nine year olds, 25% have weekday contact with fourteen to seventeen year olds and 13% have weekday contact with eighteen to twenty-one year olds. Even fewer of the benefices (7%) have any weekday contact with two to five year olds. Only 2 of the 171 benefices are able to have weekday contact with at least one young person from each of the five age bands employed in the study.

It is interesting to note that, while Sunday contact majors on the six to thirteen year age group, weekday contact majors on the ten to seventeen year olds. This presumably reflects the churches' involvement in weekday youth clubs and other groups that cater for adolescents. However, the problem of maintaining contact with these adolescents remains, as can be seen from the small percentage of the benefices which have any weekday contact with the eighteen to twenty-one age bracket. Only half the number of benefices that work with fourteen to seventeen year olds during the week continue to work with eighteen to twenty-one year olds.

One final question needs to be answered before leaving the head count attempted by this chapter. We have now formed an accurate idea of the number of young people and adults in touch with rural Anglicanism in the 171 benefices, but it would also be helpful to know how many meeting points these benefices arrange on Sunday and during the rest of the week and through which the church establishes this contact.

As we have already grown to expect from this chapter, Sunday is the day on which most of the activity in rural Anglicanism takes place, but even on Sunday the benefices do not generally seem to be overpressed with activity. Half of the benefices provide either 3 or 4 Sunday meetings, 25% providing 3 and 25% providing 4. This includes services, Sunday schools and all other kinds of Sunday meetings. At the lighter end of the scale, 17% of the benefices have just 2 Sunday meetings and 11% have only 1. At the heavier end of the scale, just over a fifth (21%) of the benefices have 5 or more Sunday meetings.

All told, a total of 591 meetings are provided on a typical Sunday in the 171 benefices. 496 of these were services, and 95 were meetings of some other kind, including Sunday schools, house groups, youth meetings and so on. By way of contrast, there are, throughout the 171 benefices, only 181 weekday meetings which attract young people. Indeed, nearly two-thirds of the benefices (63%) have no weekday meetings at all which attract young people. One fifth (20%) of the benefices offer 1 or 2 weekday meetings and the remaining 17% have 3 or more.

Implications

Two main points emerge from this simple statistical process of head counting. First, it has been demonstrated that for nearly two-thirds of the benefices the sole provision for contacting children and young people takes place on Sundays, and often then in the context of the regular pattern of Sunday services. In the majority of cases, there appear to be no opportunities during the week either to instruct the young in the faith or to provide a social context in which the friendship of the Christian community can be developed and shared with the young. This lack of weekday activity is likely to present problems in relationship both to the Christian nurture of the sons and daughters of the families who stand within the household of faith, and to the attracting of young people whose families have no contact with the church themselves. Young people who are growing up outside, or even on the fringes of the Christian community are frequently unfamiliar with the pattern of Sunday worship and the complexities of liturgy. They are discouraged by the formal environment of the church building and the services themselves. If no provision is offered for those on the fringes of the Christian community to explore the life of that community, besides the opportunity to attend Sunday worship, it is hardly surprising that rural Anglicanism is failing to make contact with new teenagers or even to retain the interest of the younger children with whom contact has already been made.

Second, it has been demonstrated that, although the rural Anglican church is still able to recruit young people after the age of five, it tends to lose them again by the age of thirteen. The fall off rate is quite steep, so that only one in every three of the nine year olds contacted by the church is in touch with the church by the age of eighteen. This fall off rate faces the rural Anglican church with two major questions. The first question is what does the church consider that it is doing in its work with six to thirteen year olds, if it is not in fact preparing them for adolescent and adult membership of the church? The second question is what does the rural Anglican church need to do in order to work more effectively among teenagers? These questions involve clear thinking about the aims and objectives of the churches' work among children and young people, the development of appropriate teaching materials for use in various church contexts with children and young people, and the training of clergy and laity for this specialist area of work.

Statistics like those discussed in this chapter help us to quantify the problems facing the work of rural Anglicanism among children and young people, but they do not of course lead us directly to understand the origin of these problems. The following seven clues are probably worth exploring.

To begin with there is the whole problem of attracting young people to take Christianity seriously in the first place. This is the key problem that faces all denominations in urban as well as rural settings. Young people are today growing up in a society in which Christianity only plays a marginal part in the adult community, and so it is hardly surprising that children and young people do not automatically come to appreciate the relevance of the churches' message for their own lives. Recent research into the attitudes of young people towards Christianity has drawn attention to the fact that young people's attitudes are today generally becoming more negative towards the church. It is against this general cultural trend that rural Anglicanism finds itself fighting.

Second, the rural Anglican churches have to be aware of the extent of the other attractions that are competing for the young person's attention. The church is proclaiming its gospel in a very competitive market place, and often to young people who are affecting a high level of sophistication. The churches need to pay considerable attention to the content, presentation and packaging of their message in order to retain a cutting edge among young people.

Third, in the sphere of secular education, a great deal of progress has taken place during the past two decades in the development of teaching materials and methods. The churches have not had access to the same kind of expertise and resources which have made possible these advances in secular education. For this reason, the churches may well find themselves operating with out-of-date educational theory and old fashioned curriculum materials, which sit uneasily alongside the expectations children have developed from their experience of secular education.

Fourth, work with children and young people requires a certain level of professional skill and a significant time commitment. On the one hand, where rural Anglicanism is losing its full time paid professionals, there seem to be insufficient lay people coming forward who have the skills and the time to develop the kind of work among young people which the rural Anglican churches need to foster. On the other hand, where full time paid professionals are still available, it is often unreasonable and unrealistic to expect these people to be able to work successfully among the whole age range of young people, since there are many other skills equally required of the rural Anglican clergy. Ways obviously need to be discovered for expanding the work of the rural Anglican church among children and young people through committed and trained volunteer leaders.

Fifth, the development of a realistic ministry among children and young people requires not only a commitment in terms of time, but also in terms of money. Historically the members of rural Anglican churches have been financially cushioned by endowments and by income earned from the investments of an earlier age. Now rural Anglicanism is having to learn the necessity to pay its own way. At present, a much larger proportion of the money raised by rural Anglicanism is directed towards the preservation of its medieval buildings than to the development of its work among children and young people.

Sixth, a special problem which the churches face in rural areas derives from the fact that there are often only a small number of children or young people within each age group living within the individual parishes. On the one hand, it is difficult to work at the same time with young people across a wide age range. On the other hand, it is often unsatisfactory to try to arrange a provision for a narrow age group when there are only one or two children likely to respond to that provision. Secular education has tackled the problem by closing small village schools and drawing children and young people together in larger schools that serve a wider rural area. This is especially the case at the secondary school level. In many ways, these schools now provide the natural reference point and friendship networks for young people rather than the individual villages from which they come. It might be helpful for rural Anglicanism to make more use of concentrating its work among children and young people on the catchment areas defined by the schools rather than on historical parish or benefice boundaries, although it is important not to under-estimate the problems of distance and transport involved in such a strategy.

The final major problem confronting the rural Anglican churches in the development of their work among children and young people is the lack of appropriate plant from which to operate. The grand buildings with which rural Anglicanism is often blessed were not designed for the kinds of needs experienced by the Christian community in the latter part of the twentieth century. Churches themselves are generally totally ill equipped for work among children and young people; parish halls are either completely lacking or often inappropriately designed and poorly equipped for work among children and young people; even where church schools exist and the churches have the possibility of using them outside school hours, the utilisation of these possibilities is often neglected; the larger parsonage houses which can offer facilities for meetings, classes and creative or recreational activities are either being sold as surplus to diocesan requirements in the light of the diminishing number of rural clergy, or being replaced by smaller and supposedly more economic dwelling units.

Against this background, possibly what is surprising is that so much work among children and young people is in fact still going on in rural Anglicanism. The job of the next chapter is to discover precisely where and how this work is taking place.

5 SUNDAY SERVICES

The previous chapter has suggested that the regular pattern of Sunday services constitutes the heart of the life of rural Anglicanism today. It is appropriate, therefore, that our next aim should be to learn as much as possible about the services that go on in the diocese on a typical Sunday.

The old service registers kept in the churches of the diocese remind us of the time, not all that long ago, when a great number of rural Anglican churches maintained the regular pattern of three Sunday services, the early morning Holy Communion, the late morning Matins, and the afternoon or evening service of Evensong. What kind of situation has replaced this old pattern as rural clergy have become responsible for more and more churches and as rural communities have become more secularised?

How many churches still have their three Sunday services, and how many churches do not even muster one service each Sunday? How many rural Anglican clergy still find themselves taking an early morning Holy Communion service in one of their churches, and how many have given up this practice altogether? To what extent is Matins still conducted as a late morning service, or has the Parish Communion movement ousted this form of Anglicanism? Is there still a place for rural Evensongs, and if so do they flourish best in the afternoon or at the traditional time of 6.30 in the evening? To what extent have rural Anglican churches abandoned the formal liturgy in favour of less formal services and so-called Family Services? What sort of congregations do the different services attract? Are there any particular times of day or forms of service that seem to have particular appeal to children or young people?

Number of services

The first point to emerge from the information supplied by the 171 clergymen is that on a typical Sunday 496 services take place in the 403 churches for which they hold responsibility. This looks as if, on average, each clergyman is responsible for conducting between 2 and 3 Sunday services. It needs to be remembered that some of the services listed in the questionnaire were not necessarily conducted by the clergymen in charge of the benefices, but on their behalf by a curate, a non-stipendiary minister, a reader or an elder.

Seventy-three of the 403 churches were offering no Sunday service at all on a typical Sunday. The complete lack of Sunday services in nearly one-fifth of the churches in the diocese can be explained in terms of the practice of small rural parishes in multi-parish benefices providing Sunday services on only certain Sundays of the month. The pattern varies very much from benefice to benefice. Some will hold a service at the same time each week, but move it from church to church. Others may arrange a pattern so that each church gets an early morning, a mid-morning and an evening service once a month, perhaps with one Sunday a month without a service.

These kinds of arrangements, while often necessary for practical purposes, raise two quite fundamental problems. First, the times and places of church services in a benefice may become a piece of esoteric knowledge, known and appreciated only by the committed few. It becomes difficult for the casual church attender to keep in touch with what is happening in his or her village, and so the irregularity of the pattern may become a deterrent for some against putting in an appearance at their local church. Second, the theory that people will move around from village to village to attend a weekly Sunday service often falls down in practice. In a number of places, the tendency remains for people only to attend services when these services take place in the church in their own community. A reduction in the frequency of services also results in a reduction in the frequency of church attendance. The rural Anglican church needs to recognise the unsatisfactory nature of the kind of spirituality into which it is training its people through the irregular pattern of service.

Two hundred and twenty-eight of the churches, that is to say 57% of the total sample, offered just 1 Sunday service. A further 57 (14%) offered 2 Sunday services, while 28 (7%) offered 3. Of the remaining 17 churches, 15 offered 4 Sunday services and 2 offered 5. Thus, the traditional pattern of 3 Sunday services is now maintained in only 11% of the parish churches in this rural Anglican diocese.

Forms of service

The most frequently available form of service in rural Anglicanism is clearly that of Holy Communion. Of the 496 services conducted in the 171 benefices on a typical Sunday, 53% of them were Communion services. The offices of Matins and Evensong were available with considerably less frequency. Evensong accounted for 19% of the total number of services and Matins accounted for 17% of them. This means that Matins was held in only 84 of the 405 churches, while Evensong was held in only 96 of them. Looked at another way, even if the majority of these services were conducted by the clergymen in charge of the benefices and not by readers or elders on their behalf, only about half of the clergy are now publicly saying Matins or Evensong with their parishioners on a Sunday. These offices can no longer be seen to be part of the backbone of rural Anglicanism today or of the spirituality of the rural Anglican clergy, at least in a public sense.

In order to complete the picture, the remaining 11% of the services so far not accounted for by the Holy Communion, Matins and Evensongs, included 41 Family Services, 7 Baptisms, 2 Complines and 5 special services.

The obvious centrality of the Communion service in rural Anglicanism today may indicate aspects both of the strength and of the weakness of the church. The Communion service very much represents the characteristic action of the believing community. The growing centrality of the Communion service may be seen as a strength in the sense that it demonstrates the way in which the rural Anglican church is providing opportunities to nurture the devotion and spirituality of the faithful. On the other hand, the centrality of the Communion service may also be seen as a weakness in the sense that it emphasises the gulf between the believing community and those outside. The Communion service is often not an easy situation in which the stranger to the church can feel at home. Indeed, some would argue that it is a most divisive way of separating out the confirmed members of the church from those who have not been confirmed. Rural Anglicanism still needs to grapple with ways of introducing those who are outside the church to this central act of worship.

Another weakness in the centrality of the Communion service for rural Anglicanism today revolves around the fact that a priest is required to preside at this service. With the continued reduction of clerical manpower, this is not the form of service which lay leadership can at present within the Church of England take over and keep going after the withdrawal of the clergy. The centrality of the Eucharist is building a clerically dominated rural Anglican church at the time when clergy are less available to maintain such a tradition. The compromise adopted in some rural benefices is for a reader to begin the Communion service and for the priest to tour several churches arriving in time to preside at the Eucharistic Prayer. This model of priesthood, which not only divorces the ministry of word and sacrament, but also minimises the personal contact between the president and the people, raises all sorts of theological and practical problems.

The way in which the offices of Matins and Evensong are receding into the background also has some important implications for the future of rural Anglicanism. It has increasingly become the case that even the most committed and regular church-going Anglicans see themselves as attending only one service on a Sunday and for the majority of them this one service is the Communion. The offices of Matins and Evensong have been able to offer Anglicanism two strengths of which contemporary Anglicans now tend to be deprived. The first strength is the recitation of the psalter and the readings from scripture. The second strength is the opportunity to give some time and weight to the preaching ministry of the sermon. The decline of the offices may well be leaving a vacuum in relationship to the use of scripture, teaching and preaching, which rural Anglicanism has not yet discovered alternative ways to fill.

The causes for the decline of the offices of Matins and Evensong in rural Anglicanism are, however, not hard to understand. The offices have their origin in the regular daily rhythm of prayer and transfer uneasily to the more spread out weekly or even monthly pattern that they have assumed in rural Anglicanism. Secondly, the way in which Anglicanism has translated the offices into choral services often requires a large congregation of people well accustomed to singing Anglican chants, preferably led by a competent organist and musical choir. Sung Matins and Evensong in a small rural congregation can be a painful experience. Finally, the offices belong to the spirituality of a believing community and tend not to serve well as an evangelistic service able to establish contact with those outside the church.

The problem of adapting the liturgy of the rural Anglican church from nurturing the faithful to reaching the unconverted is a problem that has not yet been adequately tackled, let alone solved. *The Alternative Service Book 1980* has translated the liturgy of the Anglican church into contemporary language; it has not experimented with liturgical forms better able to bridge the cultural gap between those within the household of faith and those who stand outside. In order to attempt to bridge this gap, some Anglican churches have tried to stand outside the form of services formally authorised for use and invented their own form of service. The popular name for this kind of service is the 'Family Service'.

It is interesting to observe that 41 Family Services are conducted by the 171 clergy on a typical Sunday. This is a measure of the extent to which the rural Anglican clergy feel the need to experiment with unauthorised forms of service in order to bridge the gap between their churches and the communities which they exist to serve.

The growing power of the word 'Family' in rural Anglicanism today is also indicated by the number of Communion services which are advertised as 'Family Communion'. In fact, 28% of the 262 Communion services conducted in the 171 benefices on a typical Sunday are described by this name.

Times of service

So far we have looked in detail at the type of services that take place in a rural Anglican diocese on a typical Sunday: next, we turn attention to the times at which the services take place. The first point to emerge from the data is the fact that over three-quarters of the services conducted in rural Anglican churches take place on a Sunday morning. By way of comparison, very little activity takes place in the afternoon and evening. Moreover, not only do most of the services take place in the morning, but the majority of them are concentrated into the mid-morning and late morning hours between 9.00 a.m. and lunch time.

The most popular time for services to begin is the mid-morning period between 9.00 a.m. and 10.45 a.m. A third (33%) of the services conducted on a typical Sunday begin during this period. Looked at another way, 96% of the rural Anglican benefices begin one of their services during this mid-morning period. The second most popular time for services to begin is the late morning period from 11.00 onwards. A quarter (23%) of the Sunday services begin at this time. This suggests that two-thirds (68%) of the 171 benefices have a service at this time.

The early morning services before 9.00 a.m. are also still quite popular, with 20% of the Sunday services taking place at this early hour. This suggests that nearly three-fifths (57%) of the 171 benefices have an early morning service.

Sunday afternoon is a very fallow time in rural Anglicanism. Only 34 services took place in the 403 churches in the sample between lunch and 6.00 p.m. This period of the day, then, accounts for only 7% of the total number of Sunday services. Rural Anglicanism comes back to life a little after 6.00 p.m., but not to any great extent. Eighty-four services, that is to say 17% of the total Sunday services, take place after 6.00 p.m. This suggests that just under half (49%) of the clergy are involved in evening services, and only one in five of the churches (21%) are used at this time of day.

This analysis highlights the way in which rural Anglican congregations influence the timing of Sunday services by the willingness to support them. This in turn reflects the pattern of the secular rural Sunday. The popular requirement of the 4% of the rural population who support the rural Anglican churches is a service which neither demands early rising nor interferes too greatly with their freedom for the rest of the day. The ideal time to go out to church is after a late breakfast at 10.00 a.m., or perhaps at 10.30 a.m. The problem presented by the amalgamation of several rural parishes under the care of one clergyman is that only one of the churches in each benefice is likely to be able to have its favoured mid-morning service, especially when the emphasis is on a Holy Communion service which requires the presence of a priest to celebrate.

This analysis also highlights the way in which the church buildings of rural Anglicanism, and indeed the clergymen who operate in a rural Anglican diocese, are now redundant for a large part of Sunday. The rural Anglican clergy now seem to be required in their communities as service takers not just one day per week, but merely half a day per week.

Congregations

Next we turn attention from the type and time of Sunday services to look in detail at the people who attend these services. Of the 14,321 adults who have contact with the churches in the 171 benefices on a typical Sunday, 14,269 of them attend some form of church service. This highlights how little Sunday activity goes on among adults in the diocese except through church services. Of the 7,411 children and young people under the age of twenty-two who have contact with the churches in the 171 benfices on a typical Sunday, 5,519 of them attend some form of church service. This indicates that three-quarters of the churches' Sunday contact with children and young people actually involves attendance at a service of some kind.

The total number of people of all ages who attend services in the churches of this rural Anglican diocese on a Sunday represents 3.8% of the population living in the parishes served by these churches. An important check on the reliability of the statistics produced by the present survey is provided by the fact that the statistical supplement, *Parochial Statistics of Membership and Finance 1980*, produced by the Statistics Department of the Central Board of Finance of the Church of

England, also calculates usual Sunday church attendance as a proportion of the population for each diocese. Their calculation for the diocese under review is also 3.8%. The official statistics do not, however, permit a detailed breakdown into age groups and into the times and types of services attended. Again, it needs to be emphasised that these statistics may slightly exaggerate the proportion of the population who attend church on a typical Sunday since it does not take into account the fact that some church-goers may have attended more than one service and so they will have been counted on more than one occasion.

When we look more closely at the age structure of the children and young people who attend Sunday church services, it is the six to thirteen year olds who are most in evidence. At these 496 services, there were 1,452 six to nine year olds and 1,615 ten to thirteen year olds. After the age of thirteen, there is a sharp decline in church attendance. Thus there were 1,047 fourteen to seventeen year olds in church on a typical Sunday and 704 eighteen to twenty-one year olds. By way of comparison, there were also 701 two to five year olds.

Very few pre-schoolers seem to be present in the rural Anglican congregations. This is not surprising since young people find it difficult to integrate themselves into the strange activity that is going on in church. Parents are often embarrassed by the distraction their young children cause to other worshippers. Moreover, rural churches often find it difficult to arrange crèche facilities for the young. These problems are often reflected in the fact that parents of young children tend to stay away from church, even when their inclination may be to attend. Rural Anglican churches need to find ways of accommodating pre-school children and their parents.

The ministry of the rural Anglican churches to children and young people seems to major on those middle years of childhood, when the child after the age of six is learning to participate in social gatherings involving all age groups, and before the child identifies with teenage culture. This is the time when parents begin to feel more able to bring their children to church with them. At the same time Sunday schools and junior choirs are beginning to provide an interest for this age group and to hold their allegiance. The problem which rural Anglicanism has so far not succeeded in solving is how to retain the interest and involvement of these children once they have grown into teenagers.

The next step in building up our knowledge of the pattern of church attendance among children and young people in a rural Anglican diocese is to explore the number of Sunday services which actually attract young church attenders. The most striking fact to emerge from this analysis is that one-third (33%) of the 496 services had no young people under the age of twenty-two present at all.

Looking at the presence at Sunday services of the various age groups separately, the age group most likely to be present at a service are the ten to thirteen year olds. Nearly half of the services (47%) had a young person of this age present. The next most likely age groups to be present are the fourteen to seventeen year olds and the six to nine year olds. At least one fourteen to seventeen year old was present at 43% of the services and at least one six to nine year old was present at 42% of them. Just over a third (35%) of the services had at least one eighteen to twenty-one year old present, while under a third (29%) had at least one under six year old present.

In order to assess the extent to which Sunday services were able to attract young people over the whole age range, we looked at the number of services which had at least one representative from each of the five age bands present; that is to say, at least one young person aged between two and five, one between six and nine, one between ten and thirteen, one between fourteen and seventeen, and one between eighteen and twenty-one. This condition was met by only 64 of the 496 services conducted on a typical Sunday.

The general size of the congregations attending church services in a rural Anglican diocese is quite small. About one quarter (24%) of the 496 services had 10 or less than 10 adults present, with 2 of these services having only 1 person present. Over half of the services (56%) had 20 or less than 20 adults in the congregation, while nearly three-quarters (72%) had 30 or less than 30 adults in the congregation. At the other end of the scale, there were 20 services, 4% of the total number of services conducted in the benefices on a typical Sunday, which had more than 100 adults present. The best attended service mustered a congregation of 400 adults.

The fact that one quarter of the Sunday services are dealing with adult congregations of less than a dozen draws attention to one of the major difficulties faced by the rural Anglican clergy. It is often very difficult to bring worship to life in village churches when so few are taking part. In many cases, the buildings are large and a small congregation both looks and feels lost in them. In many cases, the churches are furnished specifically to accommodate large numbers. The altar is set back against the East wall and distanced from the congregation by rows of empty choir stalls. The pulpit and lectern are set out for addressing large gatherings and consequently distance the officiating minister from the small gathering of people with whom he is trying to communicate. The singing of hymns is often difficult in small groups, and the chanting of psalms impossible, especially when the organ has been placed in such a position that the organist is unable to hear the congregation.

The problem of dealing with small congregations makes the ministry of rural Anglican churches among young people even more difficult. To begin with, young people may feel particularly uncomfortable and conspicuous in small congregations, especially if they are not themselves regular church-goers. It is difficult to make services in this kind of situation attractive to children and young people. Moreover, the majority of young church-attenders lack the feeling of being part of a large peer group: there are very few rural Anglican services that are able to attract a group of children or young people of the same age. This point really comes home to us forcefully when we examine the proportion of services in the diocese which have groups of at least 6 children within the same four year age band, and it needs to be remembered that a group of 6 children is still quite small. Only 8% of the services had a group of more than 5 two to five year olds; 17% had a group of more than 5 six to nine year olds; 18% had a group of more than 5 ten to thirteen year olds; 12% had a group of more than 5 fourteen to seventeen year olds; 7% had a group of more than 5 eighteen to twenty-one year olds. The lack of peer group support encourages the feeling of isolation and reduces the impact of the fellowship and society which belonging to a Christian community should engender. It is harder for the young on their own and away from a clear identity with a group of children of the same age to maintain the habit of church attendance.

The pattern of church attendance among children and young people is clearly related to the time of day at which the services are held. The least popular time for children and young people to attend services is the early morning period before 9.00 a.m. Well over half of these early morning services (56%) had no young people under the age of twenty-two present at all. The young people who come to these early morning services tend to be over the age of fourteen. About one in four (22%) of the 98 services conducted before 9.00 a.m. had at least one fourteen to seventeen year old present, while a similar proportion (23%) had at least one eighteen to twenty-one year old present. By way of comparison, only one in ten of these services had anyone between the ages of six and nine, and only one in twenty had anyone under the age of six present.

The most popular time for children and young people to attend services is the mid-morning period between 9.00 a.m. and 11.00 a.m. More than four in every five (83%) of the services conducted at this time of day had at least one young person present. Indeed, one quarter of the services beginning at this time have at least one person from each of the five age groups present. Looking at the age groups separately, over two-thirds (69%) of the mid-morning services had at least one ten to thirteen year old present, and nearly as many (63%) had at least one six to nine year old present. Slightly fewer (57%) had a fourteen to seventeen year old in the congregation and fewer still (46%) had an eighteen to twenty-one year old present.

Late morning services which do not begin before 11.00 a.m. are less popular among children and young people than mid-morning services, but still three-quarters (73%) of the late morning services had at least one young person present. The difference between the popularity of the mid-morning and the late morning services is indicated by the fact that about 8% less of the late morning services have any six to nine year olds, ten to thirteen year olds or fourteen to seventeen year olds present. A greater difference occurs in relationship both to the very young children and those over the age of seventeen. Compared with mid-morning services, 18% less of the late morning services have any two to five year olds present and 12% less have any eighteen to twenty-one year olds present.

Not many services take place during the afternoon and before 6.00 p.m., but three-quarters of those that do take place at this time have at least one young person present. Next to the mid-morning services it is the afternoon services which seem most convenient for young children aged five or under.

Evening services after 6.00 p.m. emerge as less popular for young people than either mid-morning or late morning services, but more popular than early morning services. In fact, over half of the evening services (55%) have at least one young person present. Understandably, very few of the evening services (5%) have any under six year olds in the congregation. One in four (25%) of the evening services have a six to nine year old, while one in three (35%) have a ten to thirteen year old, and another one in three (34%) have a fourteen to seventeen year old. Slightly less than one in three (31%) of the evening services have an eighteen to twenty-one year old in the congregation.

The final stage in this analysis of the pattern of regular Sunday church attendance is to examine the relative impact of different forms of services. It almost goes without saying that there is a strong relationship between the types of service and the times of day at which they take place. Obviously, Evensong is restricted to the afternoon and evening, while Matins is restricted to the morning. What is not so obvious, however, is that the majority (78%) of the Evensongs still take place after 6.00 p.m., rather than during the afternoon: only 21 Evensongs take place during the afternoon, compared with 75 during the evening. Matins is a service that still tends to prefer late morning, rather than early morning or mid-morning. Two-thirds (68%) of Matins still take place at 11.00 a.m. or later: there are only 26 mid-morning and 1 early morning Matins, compared with 57 late morning Matins.

A couple of generations ago, the main time for Communion to be celebrated in rural Anglican churches was the early morning. Now Communion services are to be found throughout the day. All but 1 of the 98 early morning services in the 171 benefices were Communion services, and yet this represents only 37% of the total number of Communion services celebrated on a typical Sunday. One hundred and seventeen Communion services were held during the mid-morning and 38 during the late morning. There were also 4 Communion services in the afternoon and 6 during the evening.

In recent years, it has become increasingly fashionable for some churches to call their Communion services 'Family Communion'. In fact, 27% of the Communion services discussed in the previous paragraph were described by the clergy as Family Communions. Family Communion services seem to prefer the mid-morning spot. Four-fifths (79%) of the Family Communion services began after 9.00 a.m. but before 11.00 a.m.: there were only 13 late morning and 2 early morning Family Communion services, compared with 57 mid-morning Family Communions.

Non-eucharistic Family Services are about equally divided between mid-morning and late morning, with 18 occuring mid-morning and 20 occuring late morning. Just 3 Family Services took place during the afternoon.

One of the main ideas behind Family Communion services is that they should attract more families and more children and young people. To what extent are they successful in doing this? To begin with, nearly one half (45%) of the Communion services which did not describe themselves as Family Communions had no children or young people present in the congregation at all, and only a small minority (5%) had at least one young person from each of the five age bands present. By way of comparison, only 7% of the Family Communion services had no young people under the age of twenty-one present, while 38% of the them had at least one young person from each age band present. The Communion services which consciously market themselves as being for the whole family obviously have a much greater success in attracting children and young people, and they tend to favour the mid-morning period in order to be successful in doing this. By way of a word of caution, it needs to be emphasised that the absence of children and young people from the early morning services should not be allowed to call into question the important role these early services have in fostering traditional Anglican piety among adult worshippers.

The service of Matins is by no means as moribund as the advocates of the Parish Communion movement would wish to believe. Two-thirds (66%) of the 84 Matins had at least one young person aged twenty-one or under present. More than half (56%) of the Matins services had at least one six to nine year old present, and a similar proportion (51%) had at least one ten to thirteen year old present. After the age of thirteen, the fall off again begins to happen. Less than half (45%) of the Matins services have any fourteen to seventeen year olds present, and less than a third (32%) have any eighteen to twenty-one year olds present. Matins is plainly not a service for pre-schoolers: four out of five (79%) of the Matins services have no two to five year olds present.

Evensong is less popular among children and young people than Matins. Fifty-five per cent of the Evensongs have someone under the age of twenty-two present, compared with 66% of the Matins. Practically no two to five year olds were brought to Evensong, even when the service took place during the afternoon. Three-quarters (76%) of the Evensongs had no six to nine year olds, two-thirds (68%) had no ten to thirteen year olds, two-thirds (69%) had no fourteen to seventeen year olds, and almost three-quarters (72%) had no eighteen to twenty-one year olds in the congregation.

The services which were most successful in attracting the largest numbers of children and young people were the non-eucharistic Family Services. All of these 41 Family Services had at least some children and young people present. Non-eucharistic Family Services seem particularly to attract children between the ages of six and thirteen. All except 1 of the 41 Family Services have six to nine year olds present, and all except 2 have ten to thirteen year olds present. Non-eucharistic Family Services also have a much greater success in attracting pre-schoolers than the Family Communion. Thus, 81% of the non-eucharistic Family Services had some two to five year olds present, compared with 64% of the Family Communions. On the other hand, the non-eucharistic Family Services seem much less able to retain the involvement of older adolescents than the Family Communions. Although 95% of the non-eucharistic Family Services have contact with ten to thirteen year olds, only 70% of them still have contact with fourteen to seventeen year olds. Later the proportion falls even more sharply, so that only 37% of the non-eucharistic Family Services have contact with eighteen to twenty-one year olds, compared with 57% of the Family Communion services that have contact with this older age group.

The loss of the older age group highlights the major problem faced by the development of the non-eucharistic Family Services. By often concentrating upon the younger children they tend to develop into children's services rather than into truly family services and for this reason they rapidly lose the good will of older teenagers. The idea behind non-eucharistic Family Services is to provide a form of worship acceptable to those who have not grown up with the traditions of Anglicanism and so feel lost in the Communion service or the offices of Matins and Evensong. However, unless ways can be found of building links between the non-eucharistic Family Service and the more established liturgy of the church, these services are ultimately failing in their intention of introducing new people to the life on the Anglican church. When fourteen year olds begin to tire of children's services, do they find their way naturally into the established liturgy of the church, or do they cease to be church attenders altogether?

Special occasions

Before leaving this chapter on Sunday church attendance, we shall turn attention from what happens on a typical Sunday to examine what happens on special occasions. At the end of the first section of the questionnaire, the clergy were asked to describe any special or occasional services that take place in their benefices and which attract more young people than usual. In fact 154 (90%) of the 171 clergy recognised that their churches did offer such special occasions. From their replies we can glimpse rural Anglicanism at its strongest.

A wide range of special services was mentioned by these 154 clergy. They include both non-eucharistic Family Services and Family Communion services; parade services; services for local schools; services at the main Christian celebrations like Christmas and Easter; special services for Mothering Sunday and Harvest Festival; Christingles and May Day celebrations; youth services; community services; special summer services; flower festivals and concerts.

The most common type of special service mentioned in this section as attracting children and young people seems to be the Family Service. Eighty-two of the 154 clergy who answered this part of the questionnaire said that they held Family Services in their benefices. Many of these were held monthly. Forty-three of the clergy noted some kind of special service at the main church festivals, which draw in an extra number of children and young people. Thirty-one of the benefices had occasional or regular parade services, while a further 8 benefices had special services for the uniformed organisations which they did not call parade services. Thirty-one benefices had school services, either termly or annually.

The size of the total congregations at these special services varied immensely, ranging from the smallest congregation of 14 which was a Family Service in a small rural benefice, to the congregation of 750 at the scouts' and guides' service in the cathedral. One in five of the benefices had at least occasionally 200 or more people in their congregations at special services. The sight of congregations of this size, especially when a number of children and young people are present, can give a very much needed fillip to the life of rural Anglican churches.

What is interesting to note is the fact that there are far more six to thirteen year olds at these special services than either younger or older children. Few of the services attract any eighteen to twenty-one year olds. Only half of the benefices attract any of these young adults aged between eighteen and twenty-one to their special services. In other words, the special services simply tend to attract more of the nine to thirteen year olds, who are anyway the main age group of young church attenders. The special services, like the regular Sunday services, still fail to attract the under sixes and the over fourteens.

Given the difficulty which the rural Anglican churches experience in making contact with older teenagers through church services, even special services arranged for special occasions, it is interesting to note the number of clergy who report that they sometimes try to arrange youth services specifically to cater for the older teenagers and young adults. Only 4 of the 171 clergymen in the sample try out the idea of youth services as such, and the idea does not generally meet with much success. Youth services seem to require a lot of special planning and also a firm nucleus of committed young people before they can be successful.

6 FROM SUNDAY SCHOOL TO PAROCHIAL CHURCH COUNCIL

In the previous chapter we have built up a thorough picture of the kind of services held in the churches of a rural Anglican diocese on a typical Sunday, as well as the kind of congregations likely to be present at these services. We have also broadened the picture to include a view of rural Anglicanism at its best, when the churches are celebrating the major Christian festivals or other special occasions. Throughout our aim has been to give special attention to the number of children and young people who are in touch with these services. At their most optimistic, the statistics presented in the previous chapter indicate that the rural Anglican churches can expect to have contact through their regular Sunday services with less than 5% of the children of school age living in the diocese.

Our task now is to examine more closely the ways in which these rural Anglican churches try to make contact with children and young people in addition to their attendance at Sunday services. For example, to what extent are Sunday schools alive and well in the countryside today, and to what age groups do they appeal? Do church choirs still attract a fair number of rural children, and are they willing to come out to a regular choir practice as well as to sing at Sunday services? Is there still a place for church youth clubs in the village? Is the ancient art of bell ringing still able to recruit young ringers into the towers of rural Anglican churches? And are young people given a say in the running of their local churches by being elected on to the parochial church council?

The final part of the questionnaire was given over entirely to answering questions of this sort. Once again a great deal of information was fed into the computer. In order to chart a sensible path through this detail, we shall look at the separate provisions in turn, under ten sub-headings, namely, Sunday schools, youth clubs, pathfinder and CYFA groups, church sponsored uniformed organisations, confirmation courses, house groups, bell ringing, church choirs, servers and membership of the parochial church council. Some of these headings obviously refer to provisions made explicitly and exclusively for children and young people, like Sunday schools and youth clubs. Others of them, like house groups and church choirs, examine the way in which children and young people are integrated into church activities which cater for a wider age range.

Under each of the ten headings in this chapter, we will be able to answer two different types of question. First, we will examine the number of benefices which involve children and young people in these different ways. Second, we will look at the number of children and young people in each age group reached by these provisions.

It is important to note that the actual question posed by this chapter is different from the one posed by the previous chapter. Whereas the previous chapter wanted to ascertain how many children and young people were likely to be in touch with the churches on a normal Sunday, this chapter wants to ascertain the total number of children and young people contacted by the various provisions reviewed below. For example, when a rural church says that it has the names of forty children on its Sunday registers, it does not imply that the church has contact with forty children every week. It might well be the case that this Sunday school meets only fortnightly and that less than half of the total membership turns up on any one occassion. What we are looking at in this chapter is the number of children who actually come within the orbit and influence of this Sunday school from time to time.

Sunday school

In spite of all the difficulties involved in operating rural Sunday schools, four-fifths (82%) of the clergymen in this rural Anglican diocese still try to muster at least one Sunday school within their benefice. Many of those who are responsible for more than one parish are trying to concentrate their Sunday school resources in just one parish and hope that parents from the other parishes will bring their children to the central Sunday school. Problems of distance and mobility frequently frustrate this hope.

In the present sample, 140 of the 171 benefices offer some sort of Sunday school provision. A total of 4,504 children and young people are on the registers of these Sunday schools. This means that the average size of the Sunday school register stands at 32 names, which is roughly the size of one class in a day school. This average conceals a wide range of sizes, from the smallest Sunday school with a membership of 4 children, to the largest with 170. Only 4 of the benefices have the names of more than 100 children and young people on their registers.

Generally speaking, the Sunday schools seem to appeal most to children in the six to nine year age range. Nearly half of the total number of children contacted by the Sunday schools fall into this age group. Twice as many six to nine year olds (2,144) attend Sunday school as two to five year olds (1,036). This indicates a powerful period of recruitment as children also reach the age for compulsory day school. There still seems to be a willingness among some parents, even those who are not themselves regular church-goers, to enrol their children for Sunday schools as they approach the age for attendance at day school. A number of mixed motives may well lie behind this support for Sunday school. Some parents genuinely desire church teaching for their children; some have a general feeling that Sunday school would be good for them, while others see the church as providing some sort of Sunday child-minding facility. The local churches need to be aware of the diversity of backgrounds from which Sunday school children come.

Just as there is a powerful period of recruitment up to the six to nine year age group, so there is a rapid dropping off after this age. Less than half as many ten to thirteen year olds (1,056) attend Sunday schools as six to nine year olds. By this stage, children seem to feel that they have outgrown what the Sunday schools are able to offer them.

Very few benefices have contact with young people over the age of thirteen through their Sunday schools. Only 22% of the benefices have contact with fourteen to seventeen year olds through Sunday school, while only 9% have contact with eighteen to twenty-one year olds in this way. Moreover, where such adolescents are present in Sunday school, they are likely to be isolated individuals without peer group support. Out of the 38 benefices with some fourteen to seventeen year olds in Sunday school, 10 of them have only 1 in this age group. Similarly, out of the 15 benefices with eighteen to twenty-one year olds in Sunday school, 6 have only 1 young person of this age group. Presumably, many of these young people over thirteen years of age are regarded as helpers or teachers in Sunday schools rather than as students.

While the young recruitment into Sunday schools indicates that there is still a great deal of potential in the Sunday school idea, the early disenchantment with Sunday school attendance highlights the problems faced by the rural Anglican churches with their work in this field. Moreover, the ten year olds who are beginning to drift away from Sunday school are not necessarily re-appearing in the church congregations.

Since rural Sunday schools are having success among six to nine year olds, it would seem sensible to try to build on this strength, especially since these are important years for the laying of foundations and the training of attitudes. Four things could improve the value of the church's present work among this age group. First, there is the need to make sure that those who are doing the work of Sunday school teachers have a firm grasp of the psychological needs and capabilities of this age group. Second, there is the need to make explicit the distinction between the teaching requirements of this age group and the crèche facilities required by younger children. When churches attempt to deal with pre-school children and children of junior school age range in the same Sunday school class, they almost inevitably run the risk of failing to aim at the right level to maintain the interest and good will of the older children in the group. Third, there is the need to structure both Sunday school work and the worship of the adult congregation in such a way that it is possible for the older children to graduate from Sunday school to church. I deal with this issue fully in my book *His Spirit is With Us*. Fourth, as difficult as it may seem, the rural churches need to provide an appropriate room in which Sunday schools can take place. Makeshift environments, like old fashioned church halls, cramped vestries and the corner of the church, just cannot compete for children's enthusiasm alongside the comfort of the schools in which they receive their secular education.

Youth clubs

While the majority of rural clergymen still try to operate some form of Sunday school for young children within their benefice, comparatively few of them are successful in providing some form of youth club for an older age range.

There are two different kinds of youth club which churches can try to run. On the one hand, there are those which provide primarily for the young people who attend church or whose families have some kind of church contact. Such youth clubs are consciously church-based and set out to build up the fellowship among the church's young people. On the other hand, there are those which are provided primarily for the young people outside the church. Such youth clubs can be regarded as a service provided by the church for the community, and may or may not have any evangelistic intention.

About one in eight (13%) of the benefices provide some form of youth club for young people outside the church fellowship itself. These 22 clubs cater for a total of 616 young people. This produces an average of 28 members each. In actual size, the clubs range from the smallest which caters for 10 young people, to the largest which has 87 members. Most of them are catering for between 20 and 50 young people.

The age group most attracted to the youth clubs provided mainly for non-church members consists of the fourteen to seventeen year olds. Exactly half (50%) of the young people who attend these clubs fall into this age group. The second most prominent age group is the ten to thirteen year olds who account for 40% of the total membership. The other 10% of the membership is made up of a handful of six to nine year olds and a handful of eighteen to twenty-one year olds. Sixteen of the 22 benefices which operate this sort of youth club orientate their work primarily to the over fourteens, 5 to the ten to thirteen year age group and just 1 to the six to nine year age group.

It is obvious that the rural Anglican churches no longer generally feel themselves to be in business to do community work in the form of running youth clubs which are not explicitly for the benefit of church members. While there can be no doubt that a real need exists in many of the village communities for some form of youth club, the Anglican church is being realistic in accepting the fact that it is no longer in a strong enough position to be at the centre of arranging such facilities. Secular youth work now needs to be undertaken by secular initiative. A generation or two earlier the village parson may well have had time and resources to engage in this kind of activity, but the withdrawal of the full-time clergymen from the villages has distanced the churches from this kind of involvement and from the informal contact with young people which resulted from it.

If the churches in a rural Anglican diocese have rightly decided that they cannot be responsible for the provision of community youth work, to what extent are they able to provide specialist youth work for their young church members or for the teenage children of church-going families? It is obviously as important to cater for the needs of teenage church members as it is to provide Sunday school facilities for the pre-teenagers. However, less than one-quarter (23%) of the benefices are able to provide some form of youth club for their church members.

The 39 clubs provided mainly for church members cater for a total of 932 young people. This produces an average of 24 members each. Two out of every three of these clubs are quite small, with a membership which does not exceed 20 young people. The smallest of these clubs has only 5 young members, while another 3 clubs have a membership of only 6. At the other end of the scale, just 3 of the benefices have youth clubs for church members with a membership of more than 50 young people, while the largest claims to cater for 100 young people.

Generally speaking, the youth clubs operated mainly for church members appeal mostly to the fourteen to seventeen year old age range. More than half (54%) of the total membership of these clubs is between fourteen and seventeen years of age. These fourteen to seventeen year olds are clustered together in groups, often quite sizeable in comparison with the total size of the youth club. This suggests that the culture of youth clubs is mainly orientated towards these mid-adolescent years.

While the majority of youth clubs operated mainly for church members tend to major on the fourteen to seventeen year age group, a significant proportion, two in five, orientate their work towards the younger age group, the ten to thirteen year olds. The important point to note is that when youth clubs attract these children of middle school age range, they are not also able to attract the older mid-adolescents. The parishes which try to operate a youth club for church members seem to be making a choice, either explicitly or implicitly, to concentrate their efforts on either ten to thirteen year olds or fourteen to seventeen year olds.

The next significant observation to emerge from an analysis of the age structure of the membership of the youth clubs operated mainly for church members is that very few of them have contact with young people over the age of seventeen. Only 8 of the 39 benefices providing this type of youth club have any eighteen to twenty-one year olds in them. One benefice has just 1 eighteen to twenty-one year old, 3 benefices have 2, 2 benefices have 5, 1 benefice has 6, and the other benefice has 13. It seems from these statistics that even those rural Anglican churches which operate special youth clubs for their teenage members are unable to meet the needs of young people beyond the school leaving age.

It needs to be recognised that youth clubs, like Sunday schools, can only be expected to work successfully among a narrow age range of young people. The problem faced by rural Anglican churches is that many of them only have potential contact with a very small number of young people within an age band that can successfully work together and who have an interest in church and Christianity. While the majority of benefices can muster enough six to nine year olds to make an attempt at a Sunday school, only a minority of benefices can muster enough ten to thirteen year olds or fourteen to seventeen year olds to make an attempt at a church based youth club. This has particularly unfortunate consequences for the individual teenagers living in the rural benefices who might still benefit from such provision.

In the light of this analysis, the church's work among teenagers in a rural diocese might be more successfully organised, not on a parish or even a benefice basis, but on the basis of the catchment areas served by the secondary or upper schools. Two main difficulties stand in the way of such developments. First, there is the isolation and individualism of the rural Anglican parish system: clergy are unaccustomed to working together on youth work or even to agreeing on a common policy for youth work. Second, there is the problem of transport when the young people live over a wide catchment area. Unless these difficulties can be overcome, it looks as if the rural Anglican church will continue to fail to make profitable contact even with those teenagers who might otherwise be well disposed towards the church.

Pathfinders and CYFA

The strength of groups like Pathfinders and the Churches' Youth Fellowship Association is that they offer a firm national framework on which the individual churches can build their work among children and young people. To what extent are these schemes being adopted in rural Anglican churches?

The survey data show that 29 of the 171 benefices run pathfinder groups, and these groups are in contact with a total of 563 young people. In 26 of these 29 benefices, pathfinders are operating alongside Sunday schools, presumably with the emphasis on a slightly older age range. In the remaining 3 benefices, pathfinders seem to exist as an alternative to Sunday schools.

The pathfinder groups range in size from tiny groups of 3, 5 and 6, to the two largest groups with 53 and 58 attenders. Twenty of the 29 benefices with pathfinder groups have a maximum of 20 attenders. Well over two-thirds (71%) of the young people in the 29 pathfinder groups are aged between ten and thirteen years. Twelve of the groups have some young people over the age of thirteen and 6 of the groups have some children under the age of ten.

CYFA groups exist as a parallel provision to pathfinders, catering for an older age range. However, only 12 of the 29 benefices which have pathfinder groups are also offering CYFA groups. These 12 CYFA groups are in contact with 186 young people, an average of 15 or 16 young people each. In fact the CYFA groups range in size from the smallest which has 7 members to the largest with 30 members. Only 2 of the 12 groups have a membership of more than 20. The CYFA groups work almost exclusively with the fourteen to seventeen year olds. There are no young people below the age of thirteen in these groups, and only 4 of these groups have any members over the age of seventeen.

The comparison between the relative success of the pathfinder groups and the CYFA groups again demonstrates the rural Anglican churches' failure to make contact with older teenagers after the age of thirteen. While 29 benefices run pathfinder groups, only 12 run CYFA groups. While pathfinder membership stands at 563, CYFA membership stands at 186. What happens to the young people who leave pathfinders in the 17 benefices where no CYFA groups exist? There is no evidence for significant numbers of over fourteen year olds being catered for by any other provision in these benefices.

Church sponsored uniformed organisations

Originally a number of scout and guide groups were sponsored in their formation by the church. How many rural benefices are still associated with church sponsored scout and guide groups, and how many children and young people belong to these groups? The survey data show that a total of 2,500 children and young people are in contact or potential contact with the 171 benefices through membership of church sponsored cubs, scouts, brownies or guides. This is more than half of the total number of children and young people contacted through Sunday schools. In terms of their total membership, the importance of these uniformed organisations is not to be under-estimated. On the other hand, it is only a small proportion of the benefices which have these groups within their domain.

Within the total of the 2,500 children and young people included in these church sponsored groups, there are many more girls than boys: there are 947 boys in church sponsored cubs and scouts, compared with 1,553 girls in church sponsored brownies and guides. While 25 of the 171 benefices sponsor brownie and guide groups, only 17 sponsor cub and scout groups.

The benefices which have these church sponsored uniformed organisations are able to contact through them quite large groups of children and young people. Each of the 17 benefices involved in sponsoring boys' groups is in contact with more than 25 boys, while 8 of them are in contact with more than 50 boys. Similarly, 16 of the 25 benefices involved in sponsoring girls' groups are in contact with more than 50 girls, and 2 benefices have over 100 girls in church sponsored companies.

The main age group to which these uniformed organisations appeal is the six to thirteen year olds. There are 1,005 six to nine year olds and 1,111 ten to thirteen year olds. Although the uniformed organisations loose their appeal among the older teenagers, there is still a fair number of young people over the age of thirteen involved in the movements. There are 320 fourteen to seventeen year olds and 64 eighteen to twenty-one year olds.

The actual contact which the churches have with their sponsored brownie and guide, cub and scout groups varies greatly from place to place, depending upon the sympathies of the clergyman, the group leader and the accidents of history. Generally there seems to be a great deal of potential for church involvement which goes largely untapped. Given the inadequacy of its own youth work, the rural Anglican church might be well advised to develop the potential of its church sponsored brownie and guide, cub and scout groups.

In addition to the scout and guide movements, there are the more explicitly church based uniformed organisations, like the Boys' Brigade and the Church Lads and Church Girls' Brigade. Five of the 171 benefices have sponsored this kind of group, making contact with 233 children and young people. This works out as a reasonably large average of 45 members in each benefice. The actual number of members in any one benefice ranges from 30 to 75.

These groups gain their most support from the ten to thirteen year olds. Once again, there is a rapid loss of interest after the age of thirteen. In the 5 benefices these groups appeal to 42 fourteen to seventeen year olds and 6 eighteen to twenty-one year olds, compared with 114 ten to thirteen year olds.

Confirmation courses

In the Church of England, confirmation is generally regarded not only as a sign of admission to adult membership of the church, but also as the gateway to Holy Communion. Generally confirmation is preceded by a programme of formal instruction. The length, content and value of this programme varies greatly from place to place. Quite often it is the only period of formal instruction received by Anglicans. Although there is a growing tendency for adults to come to confirmation, the majority of confirmands are still teenagers. Teenage confirmation figures provide a good indication of the number of young people taking a comparatively serious interest in Anglicanism today.

During the year previous to that in which the survey was conducted, just over half (57%) of the 171 benefices presented teenagers for confirmation. The total number of teenagers prepared for confirmation by these benefices was 746. This makes an average of 8 young people in each of the 97 benefices which presented young people for confirmation, or an average of 4 young people in each of the 171 benefices in the sample. These figures indicate the low rate at which the rural Anglican churches are recruiting teenagers into full membership. At one level, it can be argued that it is a good thing that the rural Anglican churches are no longer confirming young people as a matter of social course. On the other hand, now so few teenagers are being prepared for confirmation, it is necessary to accept the fact that a very high proportion of the young adult rural community stands totally outside the eucharistic fellowship of the Anglican church. This has profound implications for the barriers that exist between the eucharistic worship of the church and the uninitiated.

The majority of the young people confirmed come within the ten to seventeen age band. Just 47 of the young candidates were aged between eighteen and twenty-one. It seems that, if the church has not drawn young people into membership before the school leaving age, very few are attracted into membership, through the rural churches themselves, during the immediate post school years.

One of the problems faced by small benefices when it comes to preparing young candidates for confirmation is that there are often only very small groups of young people of comparable age with whom to work at any one time. Half of the benefices preparing young people for confirmation were working with groups which contained a maximum of five young people. These small groups might well contain both twelve year olds and seventeen year olds. This problem is especially acute when it comes to preparing eighteen to twenty-one year olds. Although 24 of the benefices had candidates of this age, they were generally in groups of only one or two, with just one benefice offering as many as 5 candidates of this age.

A number of clergymen are uncertain how best to work in this situation of preparing small groups of teenagers for confirmation, and they are increasingly discontented with the standard of training they can offer. At the practical level, there is a real need for the development of a graded set of confirmation training materials which teenagers can use at their own level in small groups.

House groups

House groups and discussion groups can play an important part in developing the life of the church community. For those who are already committed to the church, house groups can provide opportunities for deepening friendships, furthering study, discussing questions of faith and problems of life, and fostering patterns of prayer, worship and devotion. For those outside the church, house groups can provide ways of meeting church members and of exploring the Christian faith.

Just 88 (51%) of the 171 benefices were running some sort of house group or discussion group, but the majority of them were catering exclusively for adults. Only 25 (15%) of the 171 benefices were running house groups which included any young people under the age of twenty-two, while only 3 of them were running house groups exclusively for young people under the age of twenty-two. In most of the benefices where young people are present in house groups, they are a minority within an adult group. For example, in 8 of the 25 benefices which had house groups with young people in them, there were only 1 or 2 young people in a predominantly adult group, while in the majority of the other benefices, adults still outnumbered young people. The exceptions to this general pattern are the 3 benefices with groups existing for young people only, and these are groups of 14 or 15 young people.

Looking at the age of the young people who attend house groups or discussion groups, the majority come within the fourteen to seventeen year old age bracket. Only 5 of the 25 benefices have any under fourteen year olds in house groups or discussion groups, and 3 of them are the benefices which run groups specifically for young people. Thirteen of the 25 benefices have some eighteen to twenty-one year olds in house groups. All told, the total number of young people touched by house groups is quite small. There are 28 ten to thirteen year olds, 78 fourteen to seventeen year olds and 44 eighteen to twenty-one year olds.

One of the ideas behind house groups is that they provide an opportunity to meet informally in parishioners' houses. One of the dangers is that the groups revolve around the families who have the kind of home which can offer this form of hospitality and those who feel comfortable in accepting the hospitality offered. This model has particularly restricting consequences for teenagers still living within the parental home, since they are not free to offer hospitality themselves and often feel uncertain about their place in the kind of homes in which house groups might meet. Successful house groups for young people in the rural Anglican diocese tend to be based on welcoming and accepting parsonages.

Bell ringers

The sound of church bells is one of the phenomena most evocative of the character of rural Anglicanism. Most churches have at least one or two bells which can be rung or chimed as a way of announcing church services. The real interest and art in bell ringing, however, exists in those places where there are at least five bells and where a team of ringers can be involved in developing the complex pattern of change ringing. According to the annual report of the diocesan guild of bell ringers, 48% of the medieval towers in the diocese are equipped with a ring of at least five bells, although only a little over two-thirds of the towers so equipped are currently in ringing order.

According to the survey data, 79 (46%) of the 171 benefices actually have an active group of bell ringers and three-quarters of these groups include some children and young people under the age of twenty-two. This means that there is a total of 332 young bell ringers operating in 60 benefices, an average of between 5 and 6 in each benefice.

Bell ringing seems to attract a handful of children under the age of ten and quite a few more between the ages of ten and thirteen, but the real interest is in the mid-adolescent and late adolescent years. About half of the young people involved in bell ringing are between fourteen and seventeen years old. The next most significant age group are the eighteen to twenty-one year olds. There are 155 fourteen to seventeen year olds and 96 eighteen to twenty-one year olds. In fact, there are more eighteen to twenty-one year olds in contact with the rural Anglican churches through bell ringing than through youth clubs, house groups, church choirs or any other single provision. It seems that the close knit fellowship and the very specific purpose of the bell ringing group retains the commitment of young people better than any other church based activity.

Of course it needs to be appreciated that bell ringing often becomes a complete end in itself. It is far from unknown in rural Anglican churches for ringers to arrive to ring for morning service and then to leave, either quietly or noisily by the back door of the church just as the service is beginning. Thus, although bell ringing itself appears to maintain the interest of the age group which is most noticeably absent from the rural Anglican churches, it is far from clear to what extent this interest is directed towards Christianity itself.

Church choirs

Another feature of the design of rural Anglican churches is that the majority of them are equipped with some kind of choir stalls in the chancel, and choirs have an important part to play in the leading of singing in worship. To what extent are these choir stalls occupied by choristers? Do church choirs still provide an opportunity for young people to contribute to the leading of worship?

Nearly three out of every four benefices are able to muster a choir for some of their Sunday services, and more than two out of every four have some form of regular choir practice. Although a small percentage of the choirs do not have any children or young people under the age of twenty-two in them at all, 61% of the benefices have some children or young people in their church choirs, while half of them also have weekday contact with their young choir members through regular practices. In total, 1,235 children and young people are involved in church choirs in 104 of the 171 benefices in the sample, and almost nine out of ten of these young choristers are involved in a regular choir practice during the week. Thus, church choirs rank third, after Sunday school and church sponsored uniformed organisations, as a major point of contact between the churches and children and young people.

Most of the 104 benefices involving children and young people in church choirs also have some adult choristers. In fact, there are only 13 benefices where the choirs are composed entirely of under twenty-two year olds. A further 44 of the benefices have more under twenty-two year olds in their choirs than adult members. In other words, nearly half of the choirs have a majority of young people in them. The number of young people in a choir is generally between 6 and 20. Only 18 of the benefices have less than 6 young choristers, while only 15 have more than 20.

The age group to which church choirs appeal most is the ten to thirteen year olds. About half (51%) of the young people in church choirs come into this age group. There are over two-and-a-half times as many ten to thirteen year olds involved in church choirs as six to nine year olds, which indicates the rapid recruitment during this period. However, when it comes to the fourteen to seventeen year age group, numbers have fallen again back to the level of six to nine year olds. This fall continues so that there are only 83 eighteen to twenty-one year olds still involved in church choirs, a mere 13% of the ten to thirteen year olds so involved. A similar pattern is found in the fact that, whereas 94 benefices have ten to thirteen year old choristers, only 56 have six to nine year olds, 77 have fourteen to seventeen year olds and 41 have eighteen to twenty-one year olds.

Involvement in church choirs is, thus, quite often short-lived, appealing predominantly to the immediately pre-teenage years. A number of factors help to explain the problems which church choirs have in retaining the interest of teenagers, in addition to the general tendancy of teenagers to become less content with church life. To begin with, there is the danger that church choirs pitch their activities to appeal to the pre-teenage group. In this way, it is understandable how older teenagers feel that they outgrow the group. Then a number of rural churches have problems in finding either professional or competent musicians who know how to work with young people. Finally, teenagers need a task more interesting and challenging than the leading of well known hymns. Teenagers with a real interest in music often become frustrated by the musical limitation of their local churches.

The continued recruitment of young people into church choirs demonstrates that there is still a powerful potential in drawing young people into worship through music. At present, however, rural Anglicanism seems to lack the resources to make good use of this potential.

Servers

It is particularly those parishes with a high church tradition which have involved young people in liturgy by assisting the priest as altar servers. The survey data show that just over one third (36%) of the 171 clergymen involve children and young people in this way. There is a total of 263 children and young people acting as servers in 62 benefices, making an average of 4 in each.

The majority of these young altar servers come within the ten to seventeen age band. There are 93 ten to thirteen year olds and 116 fourteen to seventeen year olds. Just 15 of the benefices recruit severs under the age of ten. Once again, there is a tendency for the interest in serving to decline after the age of seventeen, so that there are only 37 servers left within the eighteen to twenty-one age group. Whereas the interest in church choirs falls off after the age of thirteen, altar serving seems to retain the involvement of the smaller number of young people recruited into this activity until nearer the school leaving age.

Parochial church councillors

The qualifying age for membership of parochial church councils is seventeen. To what extent are young people under the age of twenty-two elected on to the parochial church council in a rural Anglican diocese? Are young people interested in or given the chance to become involved in the decision making body of their local church?

The survey data show that 35 of the 171 benefices have a young person aged twenty-one or under on their parochial church councils, that is to say one in every five of the benefices. Twenty-eight of these benefices have just 1 young person of this age on the parochial church council, a further 4 benefices have just 2 young parochial church councillors and 3 benefices have 3, making a total of 45 parochial church councillors aged twenty-one years or under throughout the 171 benefices and 403 parishes represented by the sample.

Against the background of the general absence of eighteen to twenty-one year olds from the Sunday congregations in rural Anglican churches, the fact that there are as many as 45 young people in this age group serving on Parochial Church Councils is surely a sign of encouragement. Certainly, the election of young people of this age on to the decision making bodies of the local churches is an indication that, at least in some cases, the older worshippers are acknowledging the important contribution that young people can make to the life of the local church. This is an example which more churches would be wise to follow if they wish to draw young people into a more committed and active involvement in church life.

7 THE CLERGY

In the past, the country clergyman was in the position of being a well-known figure in the community in which he lived. By living in the community and occupying the parsonage house it was not difficult for him, if he so wished, to gain access to many of the things going on in the community. Whether they sympathised with the church or not, whether they liked the parson or not, most parishioners had the opportunity to know who he was. The amalgamation of parishes and the growth in the population in the rural diocese has the effect of creating a greater distance between the clergyman and his parishioners. If the rural clergy wish to make themselves known to children and young people, they need to find points of contact in order to establish their identity, especially in the parishes in which they are not themselves resident.

In addition to the points of contact which the churches themselves initiate with children and young people, through things like Sunday schools and church youth clubs, the clergyman is often able to make contact in other ways, for example through uniformed organisations which are not necessarily church sponsored, through local schools and through youth clubs which are not run by the Anglican church. Of course, not all clergymen have either the time or the inclination to follow up such possibilities; nor is it always certain that they would be made welcome if they were to do so. This leaves us, then, with the question as to the extent to which such points of contact are being followed up by the rural Anglican clergyman today?

The second part of the questionnaire was designed specifically to answer this type of question, by asking the clergymen to quantify their contact with children and young people on a four point scale, ranging from 'at least once a week' through 'often' and 'occasionally' to 'never'. The present chapter will examine the replies to this part of the questionnaire under the three headings of Uniformed organisations, Local schools and Youth clubs. Since one of the 171 clergymen refused to answer this part of the questionnaire, the statistics are based on 170 responses.

Uniformed organisations

There are two main ways in which the clergy can have contact with the children and young people who belong to cubs and scouts, guides and brownies. One way is when these groups come to church. The other way is when the clergyman visits the groups at their own centres. How general are such points of contact?

The survey data show that 58% of the clergymen sometimes meet brownies in their church congregation and 53% sometimes meet guides there. Similarly, 42% of the clergymen sometimes meet cubs in their church congregation, and 43% sometimes meet scouts. In the majority of cases they say that this happens only occasionally, although one in ten of the clergymen reports that this sort of contact takes place more often.

When it is a matter of the clergymen visiting the young people rather than the other way round, 48% say that they sometimes visit local brownies, and 43% sometimes visit local guides. Similarly, 35% sometimes visit local cubs and 35% also sometimes visit local scouts. Again, in the majority of cases, they say that this happens only occasionally, although one in twenty of the clergymen reports that he makes this kind of contact more often.

Three main points of interest emerge from these statistics. First, there is a great deal more contact between the rural Anglican churches and uniformed organisations than exists solely through contact with the church sponsored groups. While only 15% of the clergymen have their own church sponsored brownie or guide companies, 58% of them have brownies coming to church and 48% pay visits to the local brownie pack. Similarly, while only 10% of the clergymen have their own church sponsored cub or scout groups, 42% have cubs coming to their church and 35% pay visits to the local cub company. This indicates the extent to which positive relationships exist between the rural Anglican churches and the uniformed groups which are not church sponsored.

Second, it is apparent that the clergy are less likely to visit the uniformed organisations than the organisations themselves are likely to visit the church. In some cases, the relationship is one sided with uniformed groups coming to church, but the clergy not showing an interest in what the groups are doing on other occasions. The danger here is that no real links are established between the church and the uniformed groups apart from formal church attendance.

Third, most of the contact that takes place between the uniformed organisations and the church is occasional. Only one in ten of the clergy reports that uniformed organisations often come to his church, while only one in twenty says that he often visits local uniformed groups. Occasional contact presents a number of difficulties. On the one hand, it is unlikely that the clergy are in a position to get to know the children or young people in any real sense when they are able to see them only occasionally. On the other hand, it is unlikely that the children and young people are themselves able to build up any familiarity with the worship of the church which they attend only occasionally.

A closer inspection of the data indicates that there is a tendency for some clergymen to take a much greater interest in the uniformed organisations than others. This means that the clergymen who have contact with boys' groups are also more likely to have contact with girls' groups. Those who have contact with the younger groups are also likely to have contact with the older groups. Those who visit the local groups are also likely to encourage these groups to come to church.

While quite a lot of occasional contact is going on between the rural Anglican church and the cubs and scouts, brownies and guides, the problem faced by the church is how to make best use of this contact. The occasional parade services need to be made more relevant not only to the lives of children and young people, but to their activities within the uniformed organisations which encourage their church attendence. What would help greatly in fostering the relevance of the relationship between the uniformed organisations and the church is the development of joint projects, so that the church service could address more directly some aspect of the on-going life and work of the local company. Ideally the church service should develop out of the immediate interests and activities of the company. The need is for the church and uniformed organisation to think through and to develop some shared programme material.

Local schools

To what extent do the rural Anglican clergy make contact with their young parishioners through the local schools? How many of them are invited to conduct assemblies, or even to take lessons? How many of them feel welcome just to drop in and to make informal visits? How frequently are they to be seen on the school premises? Do the clergy tend to have contact with one type of school more than another?

The survey data show that many more clergymen are involved in primary schools than in schools that cater for older children. Indeed, four out of every five clergymen have some contact with their local primary school. The most frequent form of contact with the primary school is through informal visits. Thus, 82% of the clergy make informal visits to local primary schools at least occasionally. Fewer clergy are invited to take assemblies or lessons in the local primary schools than actually make informal visits to these schools. Nevertheless, nearly two-thirds (64%) of the clergy take assemblies at least occasionally, and over one-third (38%) take lessons at least occasionally. While a good deal of this contact with local primary schools is occasional, a significant proportion of the clergy are in fact involved with their local primary schools every week. Thus, 19% of the clergy report that they conduct assemblies at least weekly; 20% take lessons at least weekly, and 8% make informal visits at least weekly.

Involvement in middle and secondary schools is roughly equal, and much more limited than involvement in primary schools. About three-quarters of the clergy have no contact with middle or secondary schools at all. Where contact does take place, the most widely adopted point of contact is again through informal visits, with 25% of the clergy making visits to middle schools and 28% making visits to secondary schools. By way of comparison, 18% take assemblies in secondary schools and 16% in middle schools, while 12% take lessons in secondary schools and 5% in middle schools. The majority of the involvement that exists with secondary or middle schools is occasional in nature.

The clergymen's greater contact with primary schools is indicative of the social consequences of the way in which education is organised in rural areas. Although a number of small village schools have been closed, many villages still retain their local primary school, while children of middle or secondary school age travel by bus to schools in neighbouring towns or larger rural centres. Since the local primary school is often a focal point of the life in a rural community, it is a natural thing for the local incumbent to become involved in the local school, at least at the level of making regular, if occasional, informal visits. Even in the case of many local education authority schools, the local incumbent might well be invited to take occasional assemblies, and not infrequently becomes a school governor.

The middle and secondary schools tend to be much more remote from the life of many rural communites. As the children are taken away from their own villages to attend school in a neighbouring community, so they begin to lose a sense of identity with their own village. At the same time, the village church apparently begins to lose its sense of responsibility for them. Even those communities which have middle or secondary schools are aware that they cater for children from many neighbouring communities as well, and so the sense of immediate involvement in or identity with the school is lessened. Moreover, the independence of the rural benefices which define the catchment area of one middle or secondary school, together with the lack of co-operation between benefices, does not help to create the sense of contact between church and the middle or secondary schools.

The rural Anglican church certainly cannot any longer expect, as a matter of right, state schools to welcome its presence, nor can it expect to use state schools as a vehicle for evangelising children and young people. Nevertheless, it seems that schools are still generally welcoming the interest and involvement of local clergy. The levels of contact which the rural Anglican clergy have with local schools raise two important points.

First, although a large proportion of clergy have contact with primary schools, it needs to be recognised that very few of them are in fact trained teachers equipped with the professional skills needed to maximise the potential of their considerable contact with primary school children. The rural church would be well advised to investigate ways of developing its ministry to local primary schools, both by helping the clergy to understand more about the way in which primary schools work today and by developing curriculum materials which the clergy can use in a non-confessional way in the local education authority schools and in a confessional way, when desirable and appropriate, in church schools.

Second, although comparatively little contact at present takes place with middle or secondary schools, this does not necessarily reflect the idea that the rural Anglican church has no welcome or role to play in relationship to these schools. Even when schools insist that there is no place in secular education for Christian teaching, they are often keen to encourage their pupils to make an objective study of the place of religion in the local community, and to learn about the faith that other people take seriously and by which they live their lives. In order to address the changing face of religious education in the middle and secondary schools the rural Anglican churches need to consider equipping specialist resource people who are able to develop links between the church and the school community.

Youth clubs

We have already seen that only a small proportion of the benefices are actually involved in running their own youth clubs, either for church members or for the wider local community. The Anglican church is not, however, by any means the only organiser of facilities for young people. Youth clubs are also run by the local education authority, by other

Christian denominations, and by various other voluntary bodies. To what extent do the rural Anglican clergy identify with non-Anglican youth work conducted within their benefices?

To begin with, the clergy report that other Christian denominations are responsible for doing some form of work among young people in half (49%) of the 170 benefices, and a good deal of this involvement is on a weekly basis. In three-quarters of the cases in which other Christian denominations have been responsible for running youth work, the Anglican clergy are sometimes invited to take part. At one level, this indicates a great degree of ecumenical co-operation. However, very little of the co-operation actually takes place on a frequent basis. Ecumenical co-operation in youth work is thus, where it happens, generally an occasional activity, perhaps leading up to some special occasion or happening, rather than a part of the regular life of the local churches.

Just as about one in three (37%) of the rural Anglican clergy have some contact with youth work run by other Christian denominations, so a similar proportion (33%) have contact with non-church voluntary youth groups. Again, most of this contact is occasional rather than often, and only 3 of the 170 clergy claim to have a regular weekly commitment to a non-church voluntary youth group. The clerical contact with local education authority youth groups is slightly less, with one in four (27%) of the clergymen being involved in this kind of group. Once again, most of this contact is occasional rather than often, with only 4 of the 170 clergy claiming to have a regular weekly commitment to a local education authority youth group.

On the other hand, the benefices have greater potential contact with non-church youth groups through the lay members of the congregations. Thus, nearly half (47%) of the benefices have within their congregations lay people who work in local secular youth clubs. Moreover, half of the lay people who are working in these non-church youth groups do so at least once a week. The important thing to learn from this observation concerns the need for the rural Anglican church to equip adequately the committed lay people who are actively involved in secular youth work to build bridges between the young people of today and the worshipping communities of the church. This may well be a job for laity rather than clergy.

8 CHURCH GROWTH

The number of children, young people and adults contacted by the 171 benefices on a typical Sunday differ very greatly. While one benefice claims to have contact with only 10 adults, another claims a total of 665. To what extent are these differences in the number of people contacted a direct consequence of the differences in the benefices themselves, or does it all depend on whether the parishioners like the clergyman or not?

This is, of course, a difficult question to answer. We can all swop anecdotes about the successful clergyman and the unsuccessful clergyman, about the successful parish and the unsuccessful parish. But are there any underlying sociological rules which seem to predispose the church's contact in any given benefice to grow to a certain size or to be held back at a certain size? While being very careful not to forget that every benefice is unique in many ways, there are statistical procedures which can help us to understand some of the underlying patterns in church growth. What we need to do is to return to the original 171 questionnaires and to take a fresh look at them.

As well as knowing the benefices' estimated total Sunday contact with children, young people and adults, we also have some other very important information about the benefices. We know their total population, and their electoral roll figures. We also know the number of parishes in each benefice and the age of the clergyman in charge. All of these factors might well have important parts to play in determining the number of people with whom a benefice has contact on a typical Sunday. In the language of the statistician, what we need to do now is to examine how well we can 'predict' the total Sunday contact of each benefice from knowledge about the other four factors, namely the population, the electoral roll, the number of parishes in the benefice and the age of the clergyman. The extent to which this prediction works in practice is an indication of the extent to which such basic sociological factors over-ride the differences that exist in the personal relationships between the individual clergymen and their benefices.

There are two statistical procedures which are helpful in enabling us to understand the relationships between the total Sunday contact and these other factors. The first procedure is the simple one of cross-tabulation. This enables us to examine the average Sunday contact for benefices of different sizes, clergymen of different ages, and so on. The problem with this method is that it will only allow us to look at one question at a time, whether this is population or clergyman's age. The second statistical procedure is the more complex one of 'path analysis'. Path analysis enables us to look at a whole set of interrelated influences at the same time. For example, it is not fair to compare the total Sunday contact of single parish benefices and multi-parish benefices unless first we 'control' for the fact that these benefices may differ in terms of the number of people who actually live in them. Path analysis is able to take into account differences in population sizes before going on to ask whether it makes any difference whether we are dealing with a single parish benefice of a benefice made up of a group of parishes.

Because of the statistical complexity of path analysis, the detailed mathematical exposition of what we are doing has been placed in an appendix, and simply the conclusions will be repeated in this chapter itself. In this way, the mathematically minded can work at the detail of the argument in the appendix, while others may prefer to be content to assess the extent to which the conclusions of this analysis ring true from their own experience.

Population

To what extent does the number of people living in a benefice help to determine the number of people who come into contact with the church on a typical Sunday? If, on average, 4% of the population of this rural Anglican diocese come into contact with the churches on a Sunday, does this imply a straightforward relationship between population and church attendance, so that in a benefice of 500 parishioners we might expect 20 church attenders, while in a benefice of 1,000 there would be 40 church attenders, and in a benefice of 10,000 would be 400, and so on? Or is there a more complex relationship between population figures and congregation sizes?

The survey data indicate that, while there is a clear relationship between the population figures and the total number of parishioners contacted by the rural Anglican churches on typical Sunday, this is not a simple linear relationship. The data suggest that the best way to understand the relationship is to see the benefices of the diocese as falling into five different sizes. First, there are the very small benefices of under 600 people; second, there are the slightly larger benefices of between 600 and 1,500; third, there are the benefices of between 1,500 and 2,500; fourth, there are the benefices of between 2,500 and 6,000; finally, there are the large benefices of over 6,000. The point seems to be that these five types of benefices each take on their own characteristics. Because of their differences in size, they operate in different kinds of ways. It is helpful to look at each of these five situations in turn.

First, the very small benefices of under 600 parishioners are often in Sunday contact with as many as 10% of their inhabitants. The 20 benefices in the sample of this size maintain an average Sunday contact with 37 adults and 19 children and young people. It needs to be appreciated that, when these 56 people are spread over 3 services in 3 different churches and a Sunday school, the number together at any time is quite small. Because the communities are so small, the local churches need to work very hard in order to maintain the visibility and viability of their operation. At the same time, there tends to be a greater feeling of obligation on the part of the church members to support their local church. In these very small communities, the rural Anglican churches tend to struggle for survival, and the struggle seems to be rewarded.

Second, the benefices that range in population size from 600 to 1,500 cluster together to produce a coherent picture. The 75 benefices of this size in the sample were having an average Sunday contact with 55 adults and 27 children. The interesting point is that there does not seem to be a great deal of variation between the number of people contacted by a benefice of 700 inhabitants and a benefice twice that size with a population of 1,400. Although there is a slight increase in the total number of church attenders over this population range, the increase in church attendance in no way keeps pace with the increased size of the pool of parishioners on which the churches can potentially draw. Thus, in benefices between 600 and 800 inhabitants, we can expect an average of 10% of the parishioners to have Sunday contact with the church, while in the 800 to 1,100 population range the proportion falls to 8.5%, and in the 1,100 to 1,500 population range it falls further to 7%.

Once population figures rise above 1,500, there is another rapid increase in church growth. The problem, then, is to understand why it is that there is a failure for church contact to grow in relationship to population growth between the 600 and 1,500 mark. It seems to be the case that benefices below a population of 1,500 are restricted in the range of facilities which the church can offer. There are insufficient potential church members to allow the church to develop the full kind of life that facilitates growth. For example, the number and range of services is restricted; there may be insufficient people to support a church choir, house groups, youth groups, and so on. At the same time, the narrow range of facilities actually provided by the church becomes easily saturated and unable to expand to draw in new people. Benefices of this size seem to be caught between the need to stimulate fresh church involvement and the lack of a sufficiently large pool of committed parishioners to make the work successful.

Third, the most successful rural benefices are those with populations between 1,500 and 2,500. On average, the 22 benefices in the sample of this size have Sunday contact with 106 adults and 63 children, which represents something like 8.5% of the population. Being able to draw on a population of around 2,000 enables the benefices to expand their operation so much more than those who draw on a population of around 1,000. The full-time incumbent in charge of a benefice of around 2,000 inhabitants is still able to make fairly successful contact with his parishioners, and is likely to find himself working with a sufficiently large number of committed church people to be part of a successful and full church life.

The next growth in church size does not take place until the population figure rises above 6,000. In benefices of between 2,500 and 6,000, the church is likely to have no more contact with people than is the case in a benefice of between 1,500 and 2,500. The average Sunday contact of the 24 benefices in the sample where the population stands between 2,500 and 6,000 is 109 adults and 53 children, slightly less in fact than the average Sunday contact in the benefices of between 1,500 and 2,500 parishioners. The growth in population from 2,500 to 6,000 parishioners does not enable the churches to have significantly more contact with people. A likely explanation has to do with the number of people with whom the incumbent can establish effective relationships and the number of people who can co-operate together within the rural worshipping community. A church in a rural benefice of 2,000 inhabitants is able to develop to the maximum size that one incumbent and one worshipping community can sustain in a rural environment. After this saturation point further growth in the size of the community is not reflected by growth in the number of people in active contact with the church.

The fifth group of benefices are those with populations over 6,000 and these belong generally to the urbanised areas of the diocese. Churches in benefices of over 6,000 inhabitants can expect slightly more people to have contact with them than churches in benefices of around 2,000 inhabitants, but the growth in church attendance is in no sense proportional to the growth in the population figures. On average, the 29 benefices in the sample of more than 6,000 inhabitants could expect Sunday contact with 147 adults and 77 children and young people. Looked at another way, the parishes of over 6,000 inhabitants were making contact with about 2% of their parishioners. The clergy who work in these larger benefices are facing the problems of the urban rather than the rural ministry.

This analysis clearly indicates that the number of people contacted by the rural Anglican benefices on a typical Sunday is by no means simply a function of the number of people living in the benefice. Theoretically, we might have imagined that there would be a certain percentage of the inhabitants of each benefice who would be likely to respond to the gospel of Christ and become active church attenders. The data show that the real situation is not as simple as that. Different proportions of the population become active Anglicans in benefices of different sizes. Instead of a linear growth in active church members in relationship to growth in population, there is a stepwise series of progressions.

The explanation which I have advanced to account for this depends upon an understanding of the social groupings and social dynamics of the worshipping communities. I have suggested that both the size of the benefice determines what the local church is able to offer, and what the local church actually offers determines the number of people with whom it makes regular contact. On this account, the population figure needs to pass beyond certain thresholds before the rural church is able to develop certain new aspects of church life. On the other hand, worshipping communities reach saturation points through which they are unable to grow unless they are able to develop certain new aspects of church life. According to this argument, the possibilities for and limitations on church growth apply much more directly to active church membership, that is to say the number of people in contact with the church on a Sunday, than to nominal church membership, that is to say the number of names on the electoral rolls. It follows from this argument that we would expect electoral roll figures to grow in a more consistent relationship to growth in population, since growth in electoral roll figures would not be held back in the same way by the constraints of social groupings. Now, it is precisely this expectation which is confirmed by path analysis. Path model one in the appendix shows that there is a much closer relationship between growth in population figures and growth in electoral rolls than there is between growth in population figures and growth in total Sunday contact.

Electoral roll

If the electoral roll is a reliable index of church membership, there should be a close relationship between the number of names on the electoral roll and the number of people who have contact with the church on a Sunday. To what extent, then, does the number of people in contact with the church on a typical Sunday increase in proportion to the number of names on the electoral roll?

The survey data demonstrated that there is indeed a clear growth in average church attendance as the electoral rolls also grow in size. However, this is not just a simple linear growth: something very interesting happens when electoral rolls reach the 150 mark.

In the case of the electoral rolls which contain less than 150 names, the benefices can expect to have contact with about 80% of the number of names on the roll. Of course, this does not necessarily imply that the churches are having contact with 80% of the actual people whose names are on the electoral rolls, but that there is a steady growth in church contact until the electoral roll figures reach the 150 mark. Thus, the benefices with less than 75 names on the electoral roll have an average Sunday contact with 64 children, young people and adults. The benefices with between 76 and 100 names on the electoral roll have an average Sunday contact with 72 children, young people and adults; those with between 101 and 125 names have an average Sunday contact with 92, and those with between 126 and 150 names have an average Sunday contact with 115 children, young people and adults.

In the case of the electoral rolls which contain more than 150 names, the benefices can expect to have contact with only about 65% of the number of names on the roll. Thus, the benefices with between 151 and 200 names on the electoral roll have an average Sunday contact with 115 children, young people and adults, while those with between 201 and 300 names have an average Sunday contact with 164 children, young people and adults.

Why is it, then, that there should be this kind of watershed when electoral rolls reach the 150 mark? The answer might well have to do with the greater pastoral difficulties involved in caring for church memberships of more than 150 names. In the case of the larger electoral rolls, it is easier for indivduals to slip from active church attendance, without attracting pastoral attention. It seems that if clergymen can work most effectively in benefices of around 2,000 inhabitants they can also give most effective pastoral care to churches which have no more than 150 names on the electoral roll.

Age of incumbent

The average age of the clergymen in the sample is quite high. Only 13% of the 171 clergymen were under forty-one years of age; 29% were between forty-one and fifty, 30% were between fifty-one and sixty and the remaining 30% were over the age of sixty. Given the increasing demands and pressures placed on the rural clergy, is there any tendency for the older clergy either to have smaller parishes or to have less success in encouraging church attendance among their parishioners?

The survey data indicate very clearly that the problem sets in around the age of sixty. When the clergymen in their thirties, forties and fifties are compared, they reveal no significant differences either in the average size of their benefices or in the average number of parishioners they contact on a typical Sunday. The clergymen in their thirties have an average Sunday contact with 142 children, young people and adults; while those in their forties have contact, on average, with 138, and those in their fifties have contact with 147 children, young people and adults. Although the clergymen in their sixties do not generally tend to have responsibility for smaller benefices, they do have significantly less contact with their parishioners on a typical Sunday. The clergymen aged over sixty in the sample have an average Sunday contact with 84 children, young people and adults. Moreover, it is particularly in relationship to children and young people that the older clergymen experience their greater lack of success. While the clergymen over sixty years of age succeed in having contact with 62% of the adults reached by their younger colleagues, they have contact with only 53% of the children and young people reached by their younger colleagues.

How can we account for this significantly lower level of church attendance in the benefices held by the older clergy? Is it the result of there being fewer potential church attenders living in the benefices, or is it really a consequence of the clergyman's age? Is it really the case that the older clergy become less able to maintain the active church contact of their parishioners? In order to answer this question, path model one takes into account any possible differences in the population of the benefices and the distribution of single and multi-parish benefices. Only then does path model one examine whether the age of the clergyman makes any difference to either the number of names on the electoral roll or the total Sunday contact of the benefices. The very revealing conclusion of path model one is that, after differences in population and the number of parishes in the benefice have been taken into consideration, the age of the clergyman makes no difference to the number of names on the electoral roll, although the older clergymen do find significantly less people in church on a Sunday. The conclusion is inescapable that, while the older clergymen as a group succeed in maintaining the size of the nominal church membership of their benefice, in terms of the number of names on the electoral roll, they fail to maintain the active involvement of their church membership, in terms of the total Sunday congregations, as adequately as their younger colleagues.

These statistics highlight the problems faced both by the older rural Anglican clergy and by their benefices. It needs to be remembered that this older group of clergy consists not only of those who are past the retirement age, but of those who have only just passed the age of sixty. The strains of rural ministry seem to be having their telling effect well before the official retirement age.

Number of parishes

Only 38% of the 171 benefices in the sample are single parish units. This means that 62% of the clergymen in charge of benefices are responsible for more than one parish and for more than one worshipping community. To be more precise, 25% of the clergymen have responsibility for 2 parishes, 21% have responsibility for 3, 10% have responsibility for 4 and the remaining 6% have responsibility for 5 or more parishes. To what extent does the number of parishes for which a clergyman has responsibility affect the number of people with whom his benefice has contact on a typical Sunday?

The survey data show that, on average, the benefices which include only one parish have contact with 177 children, young people and adults on a typical Sunday. By way of comparison, the benefices which are made up of two or more parishes have contact with only 95 children, young people and adults on a typical Sunday. The comparison is between single parish benefices and multiple parish benefices. There is no great variation in the average number of people contacted by multiple parish benefices of 2, 3, 4 or more parishes.

At first glance, the only conclusion that can be drawn from this comparison is that clergymen in single parish benefices can generally expect to be meeting with more people in their churches on a Sunday than clergymen in multi-parish benefices. But this is only what can be expected, when some of the single parish benefices have quite large populations, while some of the multi-parish benefices may still be producing a comparatively small aggregated population. It is here that path analysis once again comes into its own, by being able to control for differences in population size before testing in a more sophisticated way whether there is a real difference between multi-parish benefices and single parish benefices.

Path model one shows that, after differences in population have been taken into account, the number of parishes in a benefice makes no difference at all to the number of names on the electoral roll, but it does make a real difference to the number of people who come into contact with the church on a typical Sunday. If a single parish benefice and a multi-parish benefice of the same population figures are compared, we would expect the combined electoral roll figures of the multi-parish benefice to be roughly the same as the electoral roll figures of the single parish benefice. However, we would still expect fewer people to attend church on a Sunday in the multi-parish benefice. This means that, if two clergymen have responsibility for the same number of parishioners, the one who has three churches to look after rather than one will have just as many nominal church-goers on his electoral roll, but significantly less active church-goers in his congregation.

This observation leads us to three tentative conclusions. First, three small churches cut less ice than one large church among the same number of parishioners and among the same number of nominal church members. Second, it is less easy for a clergyman working in a benefice of three parishes to keep the active commitment of the potential church members. Third, the clergymen working in a multi-parish benefice are likely to feel that their pastoral contact is less rewarding and less successful than their colleagues working among a similar number of people in a single parish benefice.

Conclusion

This chapter has demonstrated how some of the successes and failures of the rural Anglican ministry seem to transcend the characteristics of individual clergymen and their unique relationships with their benefices. A deeper understanding of the dynamics of church growth in the rural parishes is of considerable importance for two reasons. First, this kind of analysis can help the church to understand what is taking place in communities of different sizes and consequently to maximise the potential of its ministry in these communities. Second, the more the rural Anglican clergymen themselves come to understand about the social dynamics of their worshipping communities, the less likely they are to place the blame for the failure of their churches to grow beyond certain sizes on to their own personal inadequacy. As things stand at present, it is very plain that it is much easier for a clergyman to experience the psychological rewards of a 'successful ministry' in some rural situations than in others.

The kind of survey data available to the present project has enabled some light to be thrown on the problems and possibilities of church growth in a rural Anglican diocese. The appendix exploits the data further by examining more closely what is involved in church growth among six to nine year old children. What is now needed, in order to take the story further, is a fresh research initiative able to collect more detailed information over a greater number of parishes.

9 CHURCH SCHOOLS

In the nineteenth century the churches played an important part in the establishment of the national network of schools. Indeed, when the state first entered the field of providing funds for the establishment of schools in 1833, it did so by distributing public money through denominational bodies. It was not until the 1870 Education Act that the state set up its own secular machinery for establishing state schools in areas as yet inadequately served by church foundations. At the same time, the 1870 Education Act continued to encourage voluntary church initiative in the foundation of schools. Since the Church of England has been particularly strong in rural areas, it is not surprising that a number of rural schools were of Anglican foundation.

The 1944 Education Act safeguarded the partnership between church and state in the provision of schools. According to this act, each school originally founded by 'voluntary' bodies, like the churches, was given the choice of opting for either 'aided' or 'controlled' status. Church controlled schools became controlled by the state, but not taken over by the state. The church retained its legal rights over the school site, but was released from all financial commitment to the maintenance and extension of the school buildings. Controlled status gave the church the right to conduct denominational assemblies, appoint a minority of the managers and give denominational teaching to those children whose parents requested it. Church aided schools became aided, but not controlled by the state. The church not only retained its ownership of the school site, but also remained responsible for bearing a share of the cost of maintenance and extension to the buildings. Aided status gave the church the right to conduct denominational assemblies, appoint a majority of the managers and give denominational teaching throughout the school.

As well as safeguarding the partnership between the church and the state through the provision of church aided and church controlled schools, the 1944 Education Act also made religious education a compulsory subject in all state schools. This compulsory religious education was to be taught in county schools and church controlled schools according to the 'agreed syllabus' adopted by each local education authority. Moreover, the churches were given a voice on the committees which determined the content of these agreed syllabuses.

A number of rural Anglican dioceses, including the one in which the present study is based, decided to encourage the adoption of controlled status rather than aided status for the schools within their own area. To begin with, controlled status was cheaper. At the same time, the church tended to believe that the job of Christian education could be adequately catered for both through Sunday schools and through the teaching of religious education according to the agreed syllabus adopted for use in county schools and controlled schools.

Since 1944, the Roman Catholic church has, with only one exception, opted for aided status, and seen it schools primarily as providing an alternative system of education for the children of its own church members. As the established church of the realm, the Church of England saw itself in the nineteenth century as setting up schools for the education of the nation's children in both the three Rs and religion. After 1944 this was a task which the Church of England could do through controlled status just as well as through aided status. Indeed, even when Church of England schools elected for aided status, very few did so on the grounds of being able to offer alternative schools for the children of Anglican parents.

Another consequence of the historical development of Anglican schools in rural areas is the way in which they have tended to concentrate on provision for the younger children. While the Roman Catholic church has throughout the twentieth century continued to develop a network of secondary schools into which the Roman Catholic primary schools can feed, the Church of England, having pioneered the foundation of schools in the nineteenth century, ran out of steam as the twentieth century progressed. Consequently, as the organisation and reorganisation of secondary education has taken away the older children from the village elementary schools, so the Church of England has found itself concentrating more and more upon the education of younger children. Thus, in the early 1970s, when the three tier system of first, middle and upper schools was introduced into part of the rural Anglican diocese where the present study is based, the Church of England once again found its stake in education reduced. Having lost two year bands of pupils in the change of status from primary (five to eleven year olds) to first schools (five to nine year olds), a number of Church of England village schools suddenly discovered that they had ceased to be viable. At the same time, few Church of England rural schools were able to find the resources to expand into middle schools.

Thus, in 1980 the present diocese finds itself with 87 church controlled and 19 church aided primary or first schools, 4 controlled and 1 aided middle school, and 2 controlled secondary or upper schools. In what ways do the clergy today make use of these church schools as part of their work among children and young people? And to what extent does the presence of a church school in a benefice make any difference to the number of children and young people who have contact with.the church? In short, does the maintenance of the church school make any difference to the life of the local church?

Since there are so few middle, secondary or upper schools in the diocese, it is not possible to look at the impact of these schools on the local church in any way that is statistically reliable. We must, therefore, be content simply to examine the impact of the primary or first schools. The survey data contain responses from 72 of the 87 parishes which had controlled primary or first schools. These 72 parishes were grouped within 59 benefices. The survey data also contain responses from all 19 of the parishes which had aided primary or first schools. These 19 parishes were grouped within 18 benefices, just one benefice containing two aided schools. Conveniently, no benefice for which survey data was available contained both a controlled and an aided school. This leaves 94 of the 171 benefices in the sample without a church primary or first school of any kind.

Clergy contact with school

Chapter seven has already examined the extent to which the clergy of a rural Anglican diocese have contact with the primary schools in their benefices. At least occasionally, 81% make informal visits to their local primary schools, 64% take assemblies and 38% take lessons. Do the rural Anglican clergy with aided or controlled schools in their benefices play a greater part in the life of these church schools than their colleagues in neighbouring county schools?

We will begin by looking at the frequency with which the clergy take lessons in local primary schools. Eighty-three per cent of those with aided schools, 56% of those with controlled schools and 17% of those without a church school in their benefice at least occasionally take lessons in their local primary or first school. Weekly lessons are given by 44% of those with aided schools, 34% of those with controlled schools and 6% of those with county schools. This pattern fits in closely with the pattern for religious education established by the 1944 Education Act. According to this act, religious education in aided schools can be according to the trust deeds of the foundation and, therefore, totally denominational. Religious education in controlled schools needs to be in accordance with the agreed syllabus of the local education authority, although it is possible for denominational teaching to be given, through withdrawal classes, to those pupils opting for it. Thus the clergyman has a much more natural teaching role in the aided school.

Although a higher proportion of the clergy take lessons in aided schools than in controlled schools, almost the same proportion take assemblies in both aided and controlled schools. Eighty-nine per cent of those with aided schools and 81% of those with controlled schools take assemblies at least occasionally, compared with 48% of those with county schools. Weekly assemblies are taken by 39% of those with aided schools, 36% of those with controlled schools and 5% of those with county schools. Again this pattern fits in closely with the 1944 Education Act. According to this act, the worship in controlled schools may be conducted according to the trust deeds of the foundation of the school, and in this way the provision for denominational worship is the same in both controlled and aided schools.

The majority of the rural Anglican clergy seem to be in the habit of making informal visits to their local primary or first schools, irrespective of whether these schools are of a church or secular foundation. Thus, 94% of those with aided schools, 81% of those with controlled schools and 79% of those with county schools report that they visit their local primary or first school at least occasionally. However, those with church schools tend to be much more frequently in contact with their local schools than those with county schools. Seventy-eight per cent of those with aided schools, 41% of those with controlled schools and 24% of those without church schools make informal visits weekly or often.

Two important observations can be made on the basis of this comparison of the rural Anglican clergy's contact with church aided, church controlled and county schools. First, although they clergy have no right of access as such to the county schools in their benefices, many of them seem to receive a welcome there, with 79% making informal visits, 49% taking occasional assemblies and 17% of them even taking occasional lessons. A real relationship still seems to exist in many communities between the village school and the local church, even when the school has no formal or legal links with the church. This emphasises the way in which the majority of rural Anglican clergy need to be equipped to exercise a ministry among the staff and children of the local schools.

Second, although a great deal of contact is going on between the rural

Anglican clergy and church schools in the diocese, the rural Anglican church is still making far from full use of its potential teaching involvement in its church schools. Three of the 18 clergy who have aided schools and 26 of the 59 who have controlled schools never take up a teaching option in these schools. Similarly, 2 of the clergy who have aided schools and 11 who have controlled schools never take up the option to take assemblies in their schools. Since the majority of clergy are not qualified teachers, and some have no skills in taking lessons at the primary or first school level, it may well be a good thing that so many of them have declined ever to assume a teaching role in their local church schools. On the other hand, these statistics raise some important questions about the failure of rural Anglicanism to utilise the points of potential teaching contact with young people which are still available to the church. Indeed, appointments seem to be made to benefices containing church schools without any real reference to the clergyman's ability or interest in working with such schools. It is particularly sad from the rural Anglican church's point of view that one of the 18 clergymen who has an aided school and 11 of the 59 who have controlled schools report that they never even make informal visits to these schools.

Child contact with church

Chapter four has already made a careful head-count of the number of children and young people who have contact with the churches in a rural Anglican diocese, both on a typical Sunday and during the course of the week. The two age groups with whom the churches have most frequent contact are the six to nine year olds and the ten to thirteen year olds. Now, is it purely a coincidence that the church schools in the diocese also major on provision for younger children? Are the church schools in fact helping to recruit children into contact with the church, or is it purely a coincidence that the Church of England schools cater primarily for five to eleven year olds and that this is the age group which would naturally have most contact with the rural Anglican churches anyway?

The way to answer this question is to examine whether the presence of a church school in a benefice makes any difference to the number of six to nine year olds with whom that benefice has contact. Again, this is the kind of question that path analysis can handle. The idea is to take into account first the other factors which we already know have an influence on the number of people with whom the rural Anglican churches have contact, namely the population of the benefice, the number of names on the electoral roll, the number of parishes in the benefice and the age of the clergymen. When all these other factors have been taken into account, we can then introduce the presence of a church school into the equation to test whether this also has an influence on the number of six to nine year olds with whom the benefice has contact.

I decided to construct two separate path models, both of which are given in the appendix. One of these path models examines the number of six to nine year olds with whom the rural Anglican diocese has contact on a typical Sunday, while the other examines the number of six to nine year olds with whom the diocese has contact during the rest of the week. The comparison between these two path models is extremely interesting.

Path model three demonstrates that the presence of a controlled or an aided primary or first school in the benefice makes no significant difference to the number of six to nine year olds with whom the benefice has contact on a Sunday. Church schools are clearly not generally used by the rural Anglican churches as a way of recruiting children into their Sunday congregations or Sunday schools. On average, the benefices without church schools have just as much contact on Sunday with six to nine year olds as the benefices with church schools.

On the other hand, path model four demonstrates that the presence of a church aided primary or first school can influence the number of six to nine year olds with whom the benefice has contact during the course of the week. The presence of a church controlled primary or first school does not function in the same way. Generally, the clergy who have a church aided school in their benefice have regular contact with more six to nine year olds during the week than the clergy who have either a church controlled school or no church school at all.

The question remains, however, as to the value derived by the local churches from a situation in which the presence of a church voluntary aided primary or first school increases the contact between the clergyman and six to nine year olds during the course of the week, when this contact is not reciprocated by a significant increase in the contact made by these six to nine year olds with the church on a Sunday.

10 PARISH PROFILES –
the vicar's view

By this stage, the survey has enabled us to form a good grasp of the impact being made by the rural Anglican churches on their parishioners. We have conducted a head count of the people who come into contact with the churches, both on Sunday and during the course of the week, and we have looked in particular detail at the general pattern of Sunday church services and church attendances. We have traced the involvement of children and young people in a wide range of church sponsored activities, from Sunday schools to the parochial church councils. We have examined the contact made by the local clergy with schools, with the uniformed organisations and with ecumenical and secular youth work. We have paid particular attention to the dynamics of church growth and to the contribution of church schools. From a mass of statistical evidence we have been able to measure the life, as well as the decay, that stands behind the unchanging facade of the medieval churches of rural Anglicanism.

It is against this backcloth of statistical abstraction and generalisation that we are now in a stronger position to revert to the role of tourists, which we assumed and quickly abandoned in chapter one. The aim of the present chapter is to put some real flesh on the statistical bones so starkly exposed in the previous chapter. We shall visit just 10 of the 171 clergymen who co-operated in the survey and look in detail at their parishes. We shall visit them almost at random, and in so doing hope to meet a true cross section of rural Anglican clergymen at their work.

We shall stop first at the rural benefice of Grollingly, where the Revd George Blackwater has the care of five parish churches and 850 souls. Second, we shall move on to meet the Revd David White who lives in the vicarage at Shoreburn and looks after seven parishes and a combined population of 965 people. Our third stop is with the Revd Cecil Snow at Shillington, a small country town of 1,500 people which so far has avoided amalgamation with the neighbouring parishes. Fourth, Father Tom Freed introduces us to Bixdale, another single parish benefice in a village which has expanded quickly during the past two decades, through the development of new housing estates, into a community of 2,200 inhabitants. Bixdale church is well known in the diocese for its high church tradition.

The fifth clergyman we shall stop to meet, the Revd Owen Thornton, is one of the senior incumbents in the diocese. Now some ten years after retirement age, Mr Thornton is still incumbent of Falkwell and Almsford, two villages with a combined population of about 500 souls. By way of a complete contrast, our sixth meeting is with the Revd Tony Robbins, the young team rector of the recently formed Chattlestead team ministry. The team ministry is centred on a market town of 3,500 inhabitants and involves the six neighbouring villages.

Our seventh stop brings us to five coastal villages which form the benefice of Tyrewell, and there we meet the Revd Eric Noble. Tyrewell, with a population of 900 inhabitants, is the largest parish in the benefice, while the smallest of the five parishes, which still supports its own church, has a population of less than 30 souls. From the coast we drive into the largest conurbation in the diocese. This brings us to our eighth meeting with the Revd Norman Mills at the suburban parish of Hartfield St Mary, and our ninth meeting with the Revd Canon John Coulson at the city centre church of Hartfield St Barnabas. Finally, our tour of the parishes of the rural Anglican diocese stops at Long Barland, a market town of about 2,000 inhabitants, where we meet the Revd Kenneth Bates. The church in Long Barland is well known for its strongly evangelical emphasis and its highly successful impact on the community.

Having briefly introduced the ten benefices, the rest of the chapter will now proceed to look at them in greater detail. The reader can either follow the suggested itinerary, or visit the ten places in any order he or she may prefer. The names attributed both to the parishes and to the clergymen are, of course, fictitious, but the descriptions are all factual, based on information from the *Diocesan Year Book* and from the completed questionnaires.

Grollingley

Our first stop is at Grollingley where we meet the Revd George Blackwater, a priest in his mid-forties. Grollingley vicarage now serves five scattered rural parishes. Grollingley itself is the largest of the five villages, with a population of 275 people. The other four villages, which are spread out in a two or three mile radius around Grollingley, muster another 575 parishioners between them. The Revd George Blackwater thus has responsibility for five church buildings and a combined population of 850 souls.

Although nearly 10% of the 850 inhabitants have their names on one or other of the five electoral rolls, this still means that the nominal Anglican community in each of the villages is very small. The largest electoral roll in the benefice carries only 25 names, while another of the villages has only 14 names on its electoral roll. Interestingly, the church with the largest electoral roll of 25 names is in the smallest of the five villages, Hadingford, where there are only 120 inhabitants. Here one in five of the inhabitants can be regarded at least as a nominal Anglican.

In order to maintain a regular pattern of services in all five of these churches, the Revd George Blackwater conducts four separate services in four of the churches each Sunday. Last Sunday, he began with an 8.30 a.m. Holy Communion service at Pathtown, the church with the smallest electoral roll. There was a congregation of 6 at this service, but none under the age of twenty-two. After the early morning celebration of Holy Communion, George Blackwater just had time to go back home for a quick cup of coffee before moving on to the 10.00 a.m. Holy Communion service at Eastgate. Here there was a congregation of 10 adults and 4 children between the ages of six and thirteen. Immediately after conducting this second Communion service of the day, George Blackwater travelled back to Grollingley just in time to start the 11.15 a.m. Matins. Matins at Grollingley was attended by 5 adults and no children or young people. In contrast to Matins, the best attended service of the day was the 6.30 p.m. Evensong at Hadingford. At this service there were 18 adults, 2 six to nine year olds and 1 ten to thirteen year old.

Thus a total of 46 people from the five villages attended one of the four church services on that Sunday. This represents one in every twenty of the inhabitants living in the benefice. At none of the four services was there any contact with young childen under the age of six, or any young people between the ages of fourteen and twenty-one.

Twice a month, George Blackwater holds a Family Service, in Grollingley on the first Sunday in the month and in Eastgate on the third Sunday. These Family Services are the best attended services in the month and they succeed in attracting more children and young people, especially the one at Grollingley. George Blackwater reckons that the monthly Grollingley Family Service attracts 12 six to nine year olds, 4 ten to thirteen year olds and 1 fourteen to seventeen year old, as well as about 15 adults. At Eastgate there would be 6 six to nine year olds, 3 ten to thirteen year olds and 15 adults. It is interesting to see how the Family Services in both parishes make most impact among the children of first school age, and how the children lose interest in these services as they grow up, until there are no late teenagers attending them at all.

On the Sundays in the month when there is no Family Service in Grollingley, one of the mothers in the parish runs a Sunday school, with the help of her twelve year old daughter. At present there are 12 names on the Sunday school register, all between the ages of six and nine. The Sunday school is unable to keep the interest of the children after the age of nine. George Blackwater says that there are so few teenagers in his parish who have any real interest in the church, that he finds it impossible to make any special provisions for them. Instead, what he does is to encourage the Christian teenagers to join the pathfinders group at a larger church in the neighbouring town, some five or six miles away. He reckons that five young people from his five parishes regularly attend this pathfinders group.

Although the Anglican church runs no form of youth group around Grollingley, there is a church youth club run on a weekly basis by the local non-conformist church, and occasionally George Blackwater is invited to put in an appearance at this club. Since there are no other statutory or voluntary youth clubs in the area, the whole of the provision for teenagers seems to be offered here by the local chapel. As far as George Blackwater knows, none of his congregation are involved in any form of youth work, apart from through the local scout movement. Occasionally this scout group comes to a church service, but George Blackwater never returns the compliment by visiting the local scouts on their own territory. Neither cubs, brownies nor guides ever attend any of the five churches.

There is no contact between the churches in this benefice and the local schools. There is no church school in the benefice, and George Blackwater has no contact with any of the local education authority schools attended by the young people from his parishes. He is never invited to take assemblies or lessons in the local primary or secondary schools, and he does not see it as part of his pastoral responsibility to make informal visits to the local schools.

In fact, very little goes on in George Blackwater's parishes during the week. A house group meets once a month and sometimes attracts as many as 8 people, all over the age of twenty-one. Although none of the five churches has a regular choir, there is a group of people, drawn from several of the parishes, who come together to sing at the occasional united services, when the separate parishes pool their resources for important and special occasions, like the Harvest Festivals. Before singing at these special services, the choir will meet for a practice. This generally involved 11 adults and 2 ten to thirteen year olds. But apart from this, religion is kept to Sundays only in the churches around Grollingley.

Shoreburn

If the Revd George Blackwater seemed hard pressed to make a sensible job of his benefice of five parishes, the Revd David White has an even bigger problem at Shoreburn. At thirty-six years of age, David White is one of the youngest incumbents in the diocese, and he has also been given one of the most difficult tasks, since the rector of Shoreburn now has pastoral care over eight villages. Although one of these villages lost its independent ecclesiastical status in 1976, when the Norman church was declared redundant and the village was absorbed into the neighbouring parish, David White still finds himself responsible for seven separate parishes, seven medieval buildings and seven distinct worshipping communities.

The largest of these seven parishes is Shoreburn itself, with 300 inhabitants. As for the other six parishes, there are 220 inhabitants in Shellbridge All Saints, 200 in Shellbridge St Lawrence, 110 in Shellbridge St Margaret, 82 in Little Ratfield, 35 in Great Ratfield and 18 in Shellbridge St Cross. This makes a total of 965 souls within David White's pastoral care. All told, 12% of the 965 parishioners have their names on one of the seven electoral rolls. This still means, however, that the individual churches have quite small memberships. The largest church has 27 names on its electoral roll, while three of the other seven churches have electoral rolls consisting of 10 or fewer names.

Since his parishes are so tiny, David White does not believe that the individual churches could sustain a weekly service, even if it were possible to arrange for such a number of services to take place. His aim, therefore, is to hold three services each Sunday and to use different churches on different weeks. The pattern of worship in this part of the diocese remains traditional. Last Sunday morning David White conducted two services of Matins, one at 9.30 a.m. in Shellbridge All Saints and one at 11.00 a.m. in Shellbridge St Margaret. At the first Matins there was a congregation of 10 adults. At the second Matins the congregation was swollen by a baptism party, making 40 adults, 3 children under the age of six, 4 children between the ages of six and nine, and 2 between the ages of ten and thirteen years. The final service on Sunday was a mid-afternoon Holy Communion, at 3.00 p.m. in

Shoreburn. There were 8 communicants at the service, but no children or young people.

David White does not find that there is a demand in his seven churches for a regular Family Service. On special occasions, like Mothering Sunday, he arranges a form of Family Service, mainly for children. At a typical Family Service here, there might be 10 children under the age of six, 8 six to nine year olds and 3 ten to thirteen year olds, as well as 10 or so adults. Generally, David White finds that his regular congregation does not respond too readily to changes in their pattern of worship: they much prefer Matins. It is important to note, too, that the Family Services only really succeed in attracting children below the age of ten, and they fail completely to attract any young people over the age of thirteen.

One of the seven parishes in this benefice is able to muster a church choir which meets for a regular practice as well as singing at the fortnightly Sunday services. This choir consists of 8 adults and 3 young people aged between fourteen and seventeen. These three teenagers do not, however, generally turn up to the choir practice.

The church choir is the only point of contact between the church and children and young people in David White's seven parishes, apart from the provision of Sunday services. There is no Sunday school, no youth club, no cubs or brownies, no scouts or guides, and no house group or confirmation class for young people. David White feels that the scattered nature of the small parishes in his benefice and the conservative ways of his ageing congregation make church work among children and young people virtually impossible. On the other hand, he does try hard to have some contact with young children through the local primary school, and with older children and young people through a local non-church youth group. He says that he often visits the neighbourhood local education authority primary school. He is made welcome there, and he is invited to take the occasional assembly or to teach the occasional lesson. He also has regular and frequent contact with the youth club which is run by a group of volunteers in one of the villages.

While this rural benefice of seven small parishes is unable to sponsor any work among children or young people during the week, David White says that he is having more success working among adults during the week. At the present time, he has two regular groups meeting in his rectory at Shoreburn. There is a house group, which brings 10 adults together for study and for prayer, and there is an adult confirmation class. David White is currently preparing 3 adults for confirmation – an important sign of life and growth in what could be a lonely and disheartening type of ministry.

Shillington

After visting Grollingley and Shoreburn, Shillington presents a complete contrast. Shillington is a small country town with about 1,500 inhabitants. So far, Shillington has avoided pastoral reorganisation and amalgamation with neighbouring parishes. The vicar is the Revd Cecil Snow, a man who was ordained fifteen years ago when he was in his early forties. He feels that he is able to exercise an effective ministry in a single parish cure of this size. The parish church has 237 names on its electoral roll, representing 16% of the total population.

Last Sunday, Cecil Snow conducted two services in Shillington church, an 8.00 a.m. 1662 Holy Communion service, and a 10.00 a.m. service which he described as Morning Prayer/Family Service. At the early morning Communion service, there was a congregation of 15, including 3 eighteen to twenty-one year olds. At the Morning Prayer/Family Service, there was a congregation of 74, including two dozen children and young people under the age of twenty-two. These 24 youngsters included 2 children under the age of six, 3 six to nine year olds, 8 ten to thirteen year olds, 8 fourteen to seventeen year olds and 3 eighteen to twenty-one year olds. This means that the ten to seventeen year olds were particularly well represented in the morning congregation. At the same time as this mid-morning service was going on in church, the junior church was taking place in the neighbouring church hall. The junior church attracted an additional 26 children between the ages of six and thirteen. Last Sunday, then, at 10.00 a.m. Shillington parish church had contact with 50 children and young people and 50 adults. Cecil Snow believes that it is sensible for the church to concentrate its efforts on one well attended service. For this reason, there is no afternoon or evening service at Shillington.

Although the main Sunday service at Shillington church is usually well attended, there are certain Sundays in the year when the congregation grows dramatically and draws in many more children, young people and adults. Perhaps one of the best attended services is the end of term service held on a Sunday for the local church voluntary controlled primary school. This draws 140 children and young people, most of whom are aged between six and nine, with 10 under six year olds, 20 ten to thirteen year olds, 15 fourteen to seventeen year olds and 5 eighteen to twenty-one year olds. About 80 adults attend these services as well. Similar numbers of children and young people attend Mothering Sunday and Harvest Festival services, with slightly less under ten year olds and slightly more over nine year olds than at the services arranged for the school. A Christmas Eve Crib Service also draws about 100 children and young people, but these tend to be all under fourteen years of age. At the Mothering Sunday, Harvest Festival and Christmas Eve Crib Services there are likely to be up to 100 adults as well. Once a year, there is also a visit from the St John's Ambulance Brigade to a Sunday service.

The Revd Cecil Snow likes to keep in touch with the children and young people in his parish. He is a very frequent visitor to the Church of England voluntary controlled primary school in Shillington, and he takes assemblies there several times each term. He is not a trained teacher, and he does not attempt to take lessons in the school. After the age of nine, the children transfer from the first school in Shillington to a middle school in one of the neighbouring parishes. Although it means visiting outside his own parish, Cecil Snow still tries to visit the middle school once or twice a term. Apart from the vicar's personal contact with local schools, at least one member of the congregation is involved with a local secular youth club on a weekly basis.

Shillington is not the sort of church which operates only on a Sunday. A number of activities seem to be taking place in the parish during the week as well. To begin with, a choir of 32 choristers, who sing regularly at the Sunday services, also meets for a weeknight practice. This choir includes 8 ten to thirteen year olds, 8 fourteen to seventeen year olds, 4 eighteen to twenty-one year olds and 12 adults over the age of twenty-one. The practice is divided into two groups, the junior choir training group and the senior choir practice group.

As well as the junior choir, there are also two youth groups functioning during the week. The senior youth group caters mainly for fourteen to seventeen year olds, with a few younger adolescents and has altogether a membership of 38 young people. The junior group has about 20 ten to thirteen year old members, and 5 of a slightly older age. Although these two groups represent a significant contact with young people, Cecil Snow says that he feels uncertain about the purpose and character of these groups. He comments that, although the clubs are church sponsored, they have quickly become 'secularised' and are no longer really church affiliated. Thus, although the church youth clubs in Shillington have contact with sizeable numbers of young people over a wide age range and include the older adolescents whom so many other parishes do not contact at all, the church in Shillington is facing a problem about how to direct that contact in a positive and distinctively Christian way. This problem is highlighted by the fact that last year only 3 teenagers from Shillington were presented for confirmation, and at the present time there are no young confirmation candidates undergoing preparation at all.

On the other hand, although teenagers are not coming forward for confirmation, Shillington is not short of adult candidates. At the present time, Cecil Snow is running confirmation preparation groups for a total of 18 adults. This is a sure sign of the developing life of the rural Anglican church in Shillington, when it is able to recruit so many people of a mature age into undertaking the new commitment of full communicant membership.

Bixdale

Bixdale is another parish like Shillington which has a priest all to itself. At the heart of Bixdale there is an old village community, but during the past two decades the old village has expanded rapidly, through the development of new housing estates, into a community of about 2,200 inhabitants. The Rector of Bixdale is Father Tom Freed, a priest in his early fifties who is well known in the neighbourhood for his high church traditions. Father Tom upholds the traditional vision of the parish priest saying the daily Eucharist in his parish church and being daily available to his parishioners. Once again Bixdale is a community of an ideal size in which this kind of ministry can be exercised. When Father Tom was invited a few years ago to assume care of a neighbouring parish as well, he turned down the opportunity on the grounds that he could not adequately care for more than one parish.

Although larger than Shillington, Bixdale has a much smaller church membership. At Bixdale there are only 64 names on the electoral roll, representing less than 3% of the population. This is in part because Bixdale is not an established rural community in the same way as Shillington. In Bixdale the new estates have introduced a number of newcomers into the community who have no established links with the local church. Also, Father Tom seems to regard the electoral roll of this church as an index of active church membership: he does not encourage nominal membership.

The main Sunday service in Bixdale parish church is the 10.00 a.m. Parish Eucharist. The two features which stand out about this service are the number of children and young people in the congregation, and the way in which Father Tom tries to involve these children and young people in the running of the service itself. Last Sunday morning there were 64 people at the Parish Eucharist, and over half of them were under the age of twenty-two. There were 8 children under the age of six, 9 six to nine year olds, 12 ten to thirteen year olds, 6 fourteen to seventeen year olds and 4 eighteen to twenty-one year olds in the congregation, together with 25 adults.

Before the service began, 3 of the young people were involved as bell ringers. Then a young choir processed into the the choir stalls. Three six to nine year olds, 6 ten to thirteen year olds and 3 fourteen to seventeen year olds were involved in the choir, together with 4 adults. Children and young people were also involved as altar servers, acolytes and crucifer. Father Tom says that he is able to draw on 25 children and young people to assist at the altar: he recruits them from the age of four onwards. Another way in which children and young people are involved in the Parish Eucharist is through the church lads' and church girls' brigade which forms a monthly parade at the Parish Eucharist.

As well as the Parish Eucharist, there are two other Sunday services in Bixdale church. The attendances at these services are much smaller than at the Parish Eucharist, and they attract older people. Last Sunday there was a congregation of 10 adults at the 8.00 a.m. Holy Communion service, and a congregation of 7 adults at the mid-afternoon Evensong. No children or young people came to either of these services.

In addition to the three Sunday services, there are also regular Sunday catechism classes held in Bixdale. There are 48 names of children and young people on the catechism register, the majority of whom are under the age of fourteen. Six adults help with these catechism classes.

During the week, Mass is said on most days in the church. This happens at different times according to the day of the week, sometimes at 7.00 a.m., sometimes at 9.00 a.m. and sometimes in the evening. Usually Father Tom is joined by a small congregation of 2 or 3 and often this includes young children. The best attended weekly Mass is a 9.00 a.m. service, where last week there was a congregation of 13 adults and 4 children under the age of six.

The church's main point of contact with young people during the week in Bixdale takes place through the church lads' and church girls' brigade, which meets one evening a week in the church hall. At present, the local company stands at a strength of 42 young members and 5 adult leaders. Most of the young members are aged between six and thirteen, with 2 under six year olds and 6 over the age of thirteen.

Father Tom is a parish priest with a real concern for promoting work among children and young people in his own parish and for becoming involved in the wider network of youth work wherever possible. As well as working with his own company of the church lads' and church girls' brigade, Father Tom keeps in regular contact with the local brownies and guides, and with the local cubs, although he has no contact with the scouts. The local education authority is responsible for running a youth club in Bixdale, and Father Tom tries to show his face there from time to time as another way of keeping in touch with the youth in his parish.

Until 1968 Bixdale possessed a church school, but then a new site was needed for re-building and under Father Tom's predecessor the church decided to forgo its investment in the local school. Father Tom regrets this decison. He often visits the new local education authority first school, which is not far from his church, and he says that he is always made welcome there. Nevertheless, he is never invited to take assemblies or to teach in the school and he feels that this would be a helpful extension to his ministry among children. After the age of nine, the Bixdale children travel by bus some three or four miles to a neighbouring middle school and Father Tom sometimes visits that school as well, although it is outside his own parish.

In many ways, then, Bixdale appears to be one of those parishes in which the rural Anglican church is making most progress among children and young people. Both on Sundays and during the week, the church in Bixdale is in contact with significant numbers of children and young people, and this seems to include youngsters in every age group from two to twenty-one. It remains noticeable, however, that the real emphasis of the work is still among those under the age of fourteen. There are far fewer older teenagers involved in Bixdale church than younger children. Even Father Tom finds it easier to attract young children into the church, than to keep their interest as they grow up.

Falkwell

Some five miles or so after leaving Bixdale, driving through the winding country lanes and crossing the disused railway line, we come to Falkwell vicarage, the home of the Revd Owen Thornton. Owen Thornton was inducted into the united benefice of Falkwell and Almsford fifteen years ago, when he was already approaching his mid-sixties. Now not far from his eightieth birthday, Owen Thornton talks enthusiastically about the movement of the Holy Spirit in his two rural parishes.

Falkwell is the larger of the two villages, with just over 400 inhabitants, while the tiny village of Almsford has less than 100 people living in it. The membership of both of the village churches is very small. Falkwell has an electoral roll of 14 names, representing just over 3% of the population, while Almsford has an electoral roll of 9 names, representing about 10% of the population.

Last Sunday, the Revd Owen Thornton conducted two services, one in each of his churches. The mid-morning Holy Communion service at Falkwell had a congregation of 20 adults and 2 children between the ages of ten and thirteen. Owen Thornton was assisted in the service by an elderly server and the singing was led by a robed choir of 2 adults. Before the service a team of 6 bellringers called the people to worship with some very competent change ringing, but, having made their contribution, the ringers went home just as the service was about to begin. At the 3.00 p.m. Evensong in Almsford there was a congregation of 9 adults and no children or young people.

Although the parishes are small and Owen Thornton does not expect much of a weekday congregation, he likes to hold one mid-week Communion service. Last week was a special occasion, since the local deanery clergy chapter met in Falkwell on Tuesday morning. The usual mid-week congregation of two was augmented by seven clergymen from the neighbouring parishes.

Apart from the regular mid-week Communion service, the only religious activity to take place in Falkwell and Almsford during the week is the monthly meeting of the house group. This in fact is organised by the neighbouring evangelical chapel and the Revd Owen Thornton goes along as a member of the group, rather than its leader. The group has 15 members, but cuts very little ice among the established worshippers at the Anglican churches in Falkwell and Almsford.

During the normal week Falkwell and Almsford churches have very little contact with children or young people these days. There is no Sunday school and no youth club. There are no young people in the choir, no young bellringers, and no young people who attend the monthly house group. Owen Thornton remembers that there used to be a church-based youth club when he arrived in the parish, but then, shortly after he arrived, the person who ran the club moved away from the village and no-one else was willing to take it on. There was a Sunday school in Falkwell until much more recently, but them something went wrong and the Sunday school teacher gave up. Again, no-one else was willing to take her place. There used to be some children and young people in the church choir, but they disappeared when the choir master left.

Looking back over the year, Owen Thornton can recall three services which had been attended by more children and young people than usual. The first was the Whitsun flower festival when he reckons that there were about 8 children and young people in the congregation. The second was the Patronal Festival, when there were probably 13 children and young people in church. The third occasion was when a group of scouts was camping in the village and the scout master brought them all to church on that Sunday morning. The scouts were, of course, visitors to the parish and not part of the local community itself.

The Revd Owen Thornton is very interested in the uniformed organisations. There is a guide company in the area, but Owen Thornton does not feel that they are interested in the local church. He has tried visiting the guide company, but the group is not church sponsored and their leaders are not church people. The company has not attended a church service in recent years.

The village school is in fact a Church of England voluntary controlled school. The Revd Owen Thornton was elected as chairman of the managers when he arrived fifteen years ago, and he has served the school in that capacity ever since. He makes occasional informal visits to the school and sometimes takes assemblies there, but he has never attempted to teach in the school or to provide Anglican instruction through withdrawal classes for the children of Anglican parents.

The church school was founded in Falkwell in the mid 1850s and the presence of the Christian church has been very strong in the village at least since the foundation of the Benedictine priory there in the early twelfth century. Now, the 1980s are likely to see the withdrawal of this distinctive church presence in all but the medieval church itself. Already, the church congregation has dwindled in number and grown old in age. Falling school rolls throughout the county and the economic pressure being exerted on the local education authority are once again drawing attention to the vulnerability of Falkwell school. The school roll is now on the borderline of viability and the axe is poised. Thirty years ago there had been 9 Church of England schools in Falkwell's deanery: 7 have already disappeared and there seems little reason to suppose that Falkwell will withstand closure much longer. At the same time, when the Revd Owen Thornton retires, Falkwell vicarage will be put up for sale, and the two parishes will be added to the pastoral care of neighbouring clergymen. And so an era is about to end.

Before driving away from Falkwell, it is perhaps worth standing back once again on the village green, where we can see the school, the church and the vicarage. Are the events of the next few years inevitable, or could some other vision for the future of Anglicanism be made to work in this community?

My own vision for Falkwell has two aspects to it. The first is to see the school exerting its distinctive Anglican character. This would mean that the school would seek to adopt aided status and cease to be a purely neighbourhood school. Roman Catholic children from Falkwell and the neighbouring villages travel some miles to the nearest Roman Catholic aided first school in the local town. Strangely enough, some Anglican children travel a considerable distance to this Roman Catholic school as well in order to receive a church-based education. Could not Falkwell Church of England voluntary aided first school provide a valuable service for the Anglican families of the neighbouring villages? The second aspect of my vision is to see Falkwell vicarage occupied by a non-stipendiary priest who would earn his living from a secular job and build up the local worshipping community as his unpaid priestly contribution to the church of God. It might even by the case that this non-stipendiary priest would be earning his living in the local school. Once the school has been closed and the vicarage has been sold, the Church of England is never likely again to have the financial resources to reinstate such irreplaceable plant. In Falkwell, the alternative to decay is rapid change before it becomes too late.

Chattlestead

From Falkwell we move on to Chattlestead. Chattlestead is one of the areas in the diocese where change has been recently initiated and where experimentation is under way. A year or two ago, the three previously independent benefices of Chattlestead, Stoke Orland and Acto were united to form a team ministry. The Revd Tony Robbins, a priest in his late thirties, took up the appointment as team rector just five months ago, and he lives in the benefice house at Chattlestead itself. Tony Robbins has been joined in the team by two team vicars, the Revd Philip Steel, a man of his own age who had been one of his friends at theological college, and the Revd John Gower, an older man in his late forties. The two team vicars live in the parsonage houses at Stoke Orland and Acto. The formation of this team ministry has not saved any additional manpower or houses: its aim was more to provide the support and interchange of shared ministry.

The Chattlestead team ministry serves seven separate parishes, each with their own medieval church. Chattlestead itself is the largest of the parishes, being a country market town of 3,500 inhabitants, built around the large parish church. The next largest parish is Stoke Orland, with a population of 1,200. The other five parishes are all small villages, ranging in size from 105 to 230 inhabitants. Acto has a population of 190, Spreadingham 230, Byfields 105, Great Cernet 200 and Little Cernet 150. This makes a total population of 5,575 souls within the pastoral care of three priests.

All told, the seven churches in the team ministry have 358 names on their electoral rolls. Chattlestead church has the largest membership, with an electoral roll of 104 names, while Byfields has the smallest membership, with an electoral roll of 28 names. Looked at from another perspective, 3% of the inhabitants of Chattlestead have nominal membership of their parish church, compared with 26% of Byfield's inhabitants.

Last Sunday the three members of the team conducted a service in each of the seven churches. There were three services in Chattlestead last Sunday, and one in each of the other six churches. Sunday began in Chattlestead with an 8.00 a.m. service of Holy Communion. This was attended by 17 adults and 2 eighteen to twenty-one year olds. Matins in Chattlestead at 11.00 a.m. was attended by 30 adults, 2 fourteen to seventeen year olds and 5 ten to thirteen year olds. At the 6.30 p.m. Evensong in Chattlestead last week there was a congregation of 40 adults, but no-one under the age of twenty-two years comes to Evensong here.

The six services in the other churches were a Matins at 9.45 a.m. and a Family Service at 10.00 a.m., three Eucharists at 9.00 a.m., 10.00 a.m. and 11.00 a.m. and an Evensong at 6.30 p.m. The best attended of these six services was the Family Service at Stoke Orland. Here there was a congregation of 5 children under the age of six, 16 six to nine year olds, 10 ten to thirteen year olds and 2 fourteen to seventeen year olds, as well as 30 adults. There was also a handful of children and young people at the 10.00 a.m. and 11.00 a.m. Eucharists and at the 9.45 a.m. Matins. On the other hand, no children or young people came to the 9.00 a.m. Holy Communion or the 6.30 p.m. Evensong.

At the present time, there is one Sunday school in the team ministry, in Chattlestead itself. This Sunday school is quite a going concern. It does not begin recruiting children until they reach the school age, and it is then able to keep their interest until about the age of twelve. There are 35 children enrolled in the Sunday school, 20 of whom are between six and nine years of age, and 15 between ten and thirteen years of age. The other main way in which Chattlestead church keeps in touch with young people on Sundays is through the uniformed organisations. The local brownies, guides, cubs and scouts all occasionally come to church services. Chattlestead church choir and Chattlestead bell ringers also bring some children and young people into closer contact with the church. The choir has 3 ten to thirteen year olds and 4 fourteen to seventeen year old members. The bell ringers include 2 young men aged between eighteen and twenty-one.

The only regular activity during the week which as yet brings children and young people into contact with the churches served by this team ministry is a junior house group. Seven six to nine year olds and 8 ten to thirteen year olds regularly come to this weekly group in Chattlestead. There is no church youth club as such, no church sponsored uniformed organisations and no current confirmation classes for young people in Chattlestead. No weekday activities at all take place in the other six parishes. When this survey was conducted, the team ministry was still very much in its infancy. The Revd Tony Robbins was still new to the parishes and was far from satisfied with what he had inherited. He says that the lack of provision for children and young people 'alarms me as much as you!' But he decided that the way to start the team ministry was not by initiating a number of new activities straight away, but by quietly getting to know the strengths that already existed in the parishes and then by building on them.

While Tony Robbins had not been in the parish long enough to initiate major changes of strategy, he is trying to build up personal contacts with young people in the area through as many links with organisations and schools as possible. Already, during his first five months in the parish, he has visited local brownies, cubs, guides and scouts. He has already taken occasional lessons in a local secondary school, and made frequent visits to local primary and middle schools. He has made contact with the local education authority youth group. He also has contacts with youth work through his congregation, since at least one member of the congregation at Chattlestead is involved weekly in a local secular youth club. Thus, many personal contacts are being made and the foundations are being laid for future work. The signs are very hopeful in the Chattlestead team ministry.

Tyrewell

From Chattlestead we drive a short distance to the coast to meet the

Revd Eric Noble at Tyrewell Rectory. Eric Noble is rector of five coastal parishes. Tyrewell is the largest of his parishes with a population of 900, and next in size is Stratton Byre with a population of 250. The other three parishes are very tiny indeed. East Bay and Abbeyfield have 50 inhabitants each, while West Bay has only 30 inhabitants. When Eric Noble first came to these three parishes, he quickly realised that it was inevitable that the tiny hamlets could not continue indefinitely to support their grand medieval parish churches. In 1974 part of West Bay church was declared redundant, and now Eric Noble is hoping that the whole of East Bay church will also be made over to the Redundant Churches' Trust.

The electoral rolls of the five parishes have remained very high. Tyrewell itself has an electoral roll of 93 names, representing 10% of the population; Stratton Byre's electoral roll has 81 names, representing 32% of the population; Abbeyfield's electoral roll has 12 names, representing 24% of the population; East Bay has 13 names, representing 26% of the population; and West Bay has 25 names, representing 83% of the population. The number of people who come to church on a normal Sunday is much smaller than the number of names on the electoral roll.

Since Tyrewell is the largest of these parishes, Eric Noble arranges the pattern of his Sunday services so that there are always two services there every Sunday. Each week there is an Evensong at Tyrewell at 6.30 p.m. and the Sunday morning service alternates between an 8.00 a.m. Holy Communion and a mid-morning Holy Communion. The other four churches have a fortnightly service, arranged around a rather complex pattern.

The best attended service is the regular Evensong at Tyrewell, where there is usually a congregation of 25. The fortnightly mid-morning Holy Communion service at Tyrewell usually has 15 communicants, while the early morning Holy Communion service which takes place on the alternate Sundays draws 8 or 9 communicants. Similarly, when it is Stratton Byre's turn to have the mid-morning service there are usually 15 communicants and when it is Stratton Byre's turn to have the early morning service there are usually 8 or 9 communicants. The fortnightly services at the other three churches all have small congregations of 9 or less people.

West Bay, the smallest of the five parishes, is the only one of the group which has any regular contact with children or young people. There are 2 children of first school age who regularly come with their parents to the fortnightly service at West Bay. There is another family with 2 young children who come to the major festivals at East Bay. Apart from these two families, the Revd Eric Noble says, 'We have no children in church and no teenagers. The average congregation would be 45 years upwards'.

Although children and young people do not come to the Sunday service, two of the five villages do make some form of provision for children. Someone in Stratton Byre runs a Sunday school, and someone else in East Bay runs a Monday Club for a few five to seven year olds in the church itself. Eric Noble has no contact himself with either of these groups, and he has no idea how many children currently attend them. Both the Sunday school and the Monday Club are run quite independently from the main life of the worshipping community. They neither lead into the worship of the church nor point their pupils towards confirmation.

Eric Noble has become quite disheartened about his ministry among children and young people. He says that he has had no confirmation candidates now for three years. He no longer feels that it is really worth while preparing young people for confirmation. Looking back, he says, 'The last group of teenagers to be confirmed, apart from one or two, didn't come to their first communion'.

In spite of feeling this way about things, Eric Noble continues to make some personal contact with children and young people through the local schools and through the uniformed organisations. Although Tyrewell primary school is not a church school, Eric Noble is invited to take assemblies there quite often. Moreover, he occasionally visits the secondary school which his parishioners attend in the neighbouring town. He occasionally visits the local cubs and scouts, and he has some contact with the local education authority youth group. What he finds so sad is that his personal contact with children and young people through the schools and through the uniformed organisations does nothing to encourage them to come to his church.

Apart from visiting, preparing his sermons and chairing the parochial church councils of his five parishes, Eric Noble feels that his churches do not really need him much during the week. He reckons that, for the majority of rural Anglicans, religion has become mainly a Sundays' only affair and that the parson has generally become irrelevant to their lives.

Eric Noble's comments highlight the problems faced by a clergyman struggling to maintain the presence of the Anglican church in five small rural parishes. In this situation, it is easier to keep the services going than to convert the lives of the Sunday worshippers.

Hartfield St Mary

Driving back home on the main road from the coast, we follow the signs towards Hartfield, the county town. Hartfield is the largest conurbation in this rural Anglican diocese. Before driving into the town centre, we shall travel part of the way round the ring road. After driving past some rather pleasant between-the-wars and post-war housing development, we drop down into the less attractive area of the late nineteenth century development. Here the ring road narrows and runs between rows of terraced houses. Suddenly, on the right hand side, the row of houses is interrupted by the stark red brick neo-Gothic shape of St Mary's. St Mary's was built to a fairly tight budget in the late 1880s.

The vicar of St Mary's, the Revd Norman Mills, lives just round the corner from his church in one of the back streets which the church was built to serve. He is a man in his early sixties, who was trained at an evangelical theological college. St Mary's is by no means an easy parish, and Norman Mills has to work hard to maintain the presence of the church here.

St Mary's is a large parish, with 12,000 inhabitants. The church electoral roll carries 148 names, which represents just over 1% of the population. Last Sunday there were 108 people in church. The best attended of the Sunday services is the 10.15 a.m. Parish Communion. In last week's congregation at this service there were 3 two to five year olds, 4 six to nine year olds, 3 ten to thirteen year olds, 2 fourteen to seventeen year olds and 55 adults over the age of twenty-one, making a total attendance of 67.

The early morning 8.00 a.m. Holy Communion service and the 6.30 p.m. Evensong are less well attended and attract an older congregation. Last week there were 15 communicants at the early service and a congregation of 25 at Evensong.

As well as having some children in the congregation at the Parish Communion, St Mary's has a small Sunday school. Last week 5 children below the age of six and 8 six to nine year olds came to the Sunday school. The Sunday school is run by 4 adults and 2 older teenagers who take it in turns to prepare lessons. Going through his diary for the rest of the week, Norman Mills demonstrates that St Mary's is really quite an active parish, especially in comparison with many of the rural churches in the diocese. Monday is the vicar's day off, so nothing much happens then. On Tuesday afternoon, Norman Mills pays a visit to the sewing party which is attended by 15 ladies. On Tuesday evening he goes along to the choir practice. St Mary's has a small choir, involving 2 children under the age of ten, 2 ten to thirteen year olds and 2 fourteen to seventeen year olds, together with 4 adults. On Wednesday morning, Norman Mills conducts two Communion services in the homes of those who cannot come to church. The first service is at 9.30 a.m. for 3 elderly residents at a local old people's home, while the second is in a private house for just 2 adults. On Wednesday evening he is involved in a prayer group which has 7 regular attenders. On Thursday morning there is a mid-week Communion service in St Mary's church. Last week 9 adults came to this service. On Thursday evening Norman Mills takes part in the church men's meeting. Last week this was attended by 23 men.

Friday evening is youth club time. St Mary's runs a youth club mainly for non-church members, with the aim of introducing them to the fellowship of the church. Currently the youth club has 18 members, 5 of whom were recently confirmed. Last week 14 of the members turned up to the meeting, 6 of whom were under the age of fourteen and the remaining 8 were between the ages of fourteen and seventeen. Six adults take it in turns to run the youth club, with 3 or 4 of them coming to each meeting.

One of the main ways by which St Mary's keeps in touch with children and young people is through the uniformed organisations. St Mary's has church sponsored groups for both boys and girls. The church sponsored cubs and scouts have a membership of 15 six to nine year olds, 20 ten to thirteen year olds and 5 fourteen to seventeen year olds, making a total of 40 young people under the leadership of 3 adults. The church sponsored brownies and guides have a membership of 8 six to nine year olds, 7 ten to thirteen year olds, 3 fourteen to seventeen year olds and 2 eighteen to twenty-one year olds, making a total of 20 young people under the leadership of 2 adults. Although Norman Mills is not able to visit each of these groups every week, he tries to keep in close contact with them. Once a month these church sponsored organisations come to a church parade service. About half the total number of young people in the companies turn up to these parade services. There are usually 20 or so extra adults in the congregation on this Sunday as well, since some of the children and young people bring their parents along with them. St Mary's is one of those churches which has continued to invest a lot of energy in its church sponsored cubs and scouts and its church sponsored brownies and guides, and consequently continues to reap some benefit from its association with these groups.

The other regular point of contact between St Mary's church and children is the regular weekly visit which the vicar makes to the neighbourhood local education authority primary school. The school never invites him to take assemblies or to teach, but he is always made to feel most welcome in the school. In this way he gets to know a number of the young children.

An urban ministry in this kind of parish is no easy undertaking. While the church life at St Mary's seems so much fuller than the life of many rural benefices in the diocese, the Revd Norman Mills remains very conscious that his church is touching the lives of only a minute proportion of the 12,000 people who live in the parish.

Hartfield St Barnabas

Before leaving the county town, we will go right into the city centre to visit the medieval parish of St Barnabas and to meet the rector, the Revd Canon John Coulson. Although only a 20 minute walk separates St Barnabas' church in the city centre from St Mary's church on the ring road, the characters of these two parishes differ greatly from each other. Situated right in the city centre, St Barnabas' parish has been taken over by shopping precincts and office buildings, while the population has moved out into the suburbs.

Canon Coulson is a priest in his early fifties. He has been rector of St Barnabas' for seven or eight years, and has enjoyed the challenge and prestige of being responsible for the principal city centre church in Hartfield. His ministry here is quite different from that of the majority of parish priests in the diocese. In his own words, 'St Barnabas has a very small legal parish, with only about 30 inhabitants. So we have an "eclectic" congregation, drawn from the whole of Hartfield and the surrounding area.' With only 30 inhabitants, St Barnabas is one of the smallest parishes in the diocese. On the other hand, St Barnabas' electoral roll carries 350 names, giving it one of the largest church memberships in the diocese.

On a typical Sunday, Canon Coulson conducts four services in St Barnabas' church. Sunday begins with the traditional 8.00 a.m. Holy Communion service. Then at 9.45 a.m. there is the Family Communion service and at 11.00 a.m. there is the Choral Communion service. Sunday finishes with a sung Evensong and sermon at 6.30 p.m. By far the best attended of the Sunday services is the mid-morning Family Communion. Last week at the Family Communion there was a congregation of 120 adults and 75 children and young people. Unlike so many Family Communion services, the service at St Barnabas is able to attract the whole age range of children and young people. Last week the

75 children and young people included 5 two to five year olds, 15 six to nine year olds, 20 ten to thirteen year olds, 20 fourteen to seventeen year olds and 15 eighteen to twenty-one year olds.

The early morning Holy Communion is a quiet affair, which generally has a congregation of about 20 adults. This is not the kind of service that attracts any children, teenagers or young adults. The late morning Choral Communion generally expects a congregation of between 60 and 70. Last week there were 35 adults and 30 children and young people, including 10 six to nine year olds, 10 ten to thirteen year olds and 10 fourteen to seventeen year olds. Evensong has a similar size of congregation to the Choral Communion. Last week about 35 adults, 5 eighteen to twenty-one year olds, 5 fourteen to seventeen year olds, 10 ten to thirteen year olds and 10 six to nine year olds attended Evensong.

St Barnabas has a good musical tradition. It is the kind of city centre church which arranges lunch time organ recitals and evening concerts during the week. Canon Coulson describes the Sunday Choral Communion and Evensong as 'cathedral type' services. Consequently, the choir of St Barnabas is of quite a high standard and includes a number of children and young people who take music seriously. Currently the choir consists of 8 ten to thirteen year olds, 8 fourteen to seventeen year olds, 4 eighteen to twenty-one year olds and 12 adults.

As well as through the choir, the worship of St Barnabas involves young people both as altar servers and as bell ringers. Currently, there are 4 young servers aged between fourteen and seventeen, as well as 2 adult servers. There are also 8 young bell ringers aged between fourteen and twenty-one, as well as 8 adult bell ringers.

St Barnabas is an active church during the week as well as on Sundays. Last week there had been several small confirmation classes, catering for 17 people, including 7 ten to thirteen year olds, 6 fourteen to seventeen year olds and 4 adults over the age of twenty-one. There were also several house groups during the week, involving 30 adults. Usually two youth clubs also meet during the week, one catering mainly for church members and the other catering mainly for young people outside the church. Last week, however, the two youth clubs had pooled their resources to take part in a special evening of folk music in the churchyard. Fifty young people had come along to this evening, as well as a few adults.

St Barnabas is regarded by the people of Hartfield as a kind of civic church, with the consequence that a number of city events and functions take place around St Barnabas' church. For example, last week Hartfield School held its annual commemoration service in St

Barnabas' church, and crowded the church with 800 young people of secondary school age, in addition to a number of parents and former pupils. At the same time, the ministry of St Barnabas' church often extends beyond the city itself. Canon Coulson says that 'we are often asked to host diocesan and county services'. By gaining a reputation as a centre for 'worship and the arts', St Barnabas often attracts visitors from over a wide area.

Thus, as a direct result of its position and its lack of resident parishioners, St Barnabas has created for itself a unique ministry of hospitality to the county town and to the wider area. As well as maintaining a high standard of Sunday services and a valuable teaching ministry, St Barnabas is making contact with many people through civic services, concerts and other events. St Barnabas is encouraging valuable links between the Anglican church and the city, between the Anglican church and schools, and between the Anglican church and the arts. The more regular and planned interchange between a city centre church like this and some of the small rural parishes of the diocese could offer quite a lot of support and encouragement to those small worshipping communities which sometimes become so discouraged by their very isolation. It could be particularly beneficial for the individual teenagers who have stayed with their village churches to be able to identify from time to time with a group of committed Christians of their own age through some sort of recognised association with a church like St Barnabas.

Long Barland

After leaving Hartfield, our final stop on the way home is at Long Barland, a small country market town. Long Barland is situated on a picturesque river, about ten miles from the coast. With a population of about 2,000, Long Barland has so far not been forced into an amalgamation with any of its neighbouring parishes. The vicar of Long Barland, the Revd Kenneth Bates, a man in his late forties, runs his parish in a firm evangelical tradition. Long Barland church has an electoral roll of 255 names, representing nearly 12% of the population.

Kenneth Bates holds three services every Sunday in Long Barland church, an 8.00 a.m. Holy Communion, a 10.30 a.m. Parish Communion and a 6.30 p.m. Evensong. Of these three services, it is the mid-morning Parish Communion which attracts the largest congregation. In particular, this service makes a lot of impact among children and young people. Last week there were 68 adults and 102 children and young people at this mid-morning service. Looking more closely at the age structure of the children and young people at this service, there were 15 two to five year olds, 24 six to nine year olds, 23 ten to thirteen year olds, 20 fourteen to seventeen year olds and 20 eighteen to twenty-one year olds. Young people help at this service both as bell ringers and as choristers. The bell ringing team includes 4 fourteen to seventeen year olds and 2 eighteen to twenty-one year olds, as well as 6 adults. The choir includes 4 ten to thirteen year olds, 4 fourteen to seventeen year olds and 6 eighteen to twenty-one year olds, as well as 8 adults.

At the early morning Holy Communion service last Sunday, there was a congregation of 21, including 3 young people between the ages of eighteen and twenty-one. At Evensong last Sunday there was a congregation of 50. This was made up by 2 six to nine year olds, 6 fourteen to seventeen year olds, 6 eighteen to twenty-one year olds and 36 adults.

As well as the three services, there are two other groups which meet on Sundays especially for children and young people. On Sunday morning, there is a Sunday school for children up to the age of thirteen. All told there are 90 names on the Sunday school register, including 20 infants under the age of six, 40 six to nine year olds and 30 ten to thirteen year olds. On Sunday evening, after Evensong, there is a meeting of the young people's choir for teenagers. This choir is quite distinct from the choir which sings at the church services, although there is some overlap between the membership of the two choirs. The youth choir consists of 12 fourteen to seventeen year olds and 16 eighteen to twenty-one year olds.

The Revd Kenneth Bates believes that his ministry among children and young people is one of the most important aspects of his work as vicar of Long Barland. Last week he was involved with various aspects of his church's work among children and young people on four consecutive evenings. On Monday evening, Kenneth Bates ran two confirmation classes. The first confirmation group, at 6.30 p.m., was for 4 ten to thirteen year olds, while the second group, at 7.30 p.m., was for 10 fourteen to seventeen year olds. On Tuesday evening, Kenneth Bates took part in the pathfinders group at 6.00 p.m. The pathfinders group involves 30 ten to thirteen year olds, as well as 2 late teenagers and 5 adults who act as leaders. After pathfinders on Tuesday, at 8.00 p.m., there was a meeting for church teachers. Nine people came to this meeting, including 3 teenagers under the age of eighteen and 4 between the ages of eighteen and twenty-one. This indicates the extent to which young people are encouraged to exercise some leadership in the church at Long Barland. On Wednesday evening, at 7.30 p.m., there was a meeting of the church youth council. The church youth council involves 20 young people aged twenty-one or under and 2 over the age of twenty-one. On Thursday evening, Kenneth Bates went along to the regular church choir practice at 6.45 p.m., where once again he was in contact with a number of young people.

In addition to the meetings which Kenneth Bates was able to attend himself, Long Barland church runs a number of other groups for children and young people. To begin with, there are two youth clubs, both involving about 30 fourteen to seventeen year olds. One is operated mainly for church members, while the other is operated mainly for non-church members. There is also an older youth fellowship catering for 25 eighteen to twenty-five year olds. There is a CYFA group involving 30 fourteen to seventeen year olds. There are house groups and discussion groups, involving about 20 fourteen to seventeen year olds, 20 eighteen to twenty-one year olds and 20 adults. There are also church sponsored cubs and brownies, with which the church has close links. The cubs involve 34 young boys and the brownies involve 30 young girls.

During the summer holidays, Long Barland runs a series of programmes for children and young people in order to involve them more fully in the life of the local church. The programmes are intended both to be enjoyable and to be evangelical. To begin with, there is a summer holiday club for children between the ages of about four and ten. This is run for a week in the vicarage garden, during the early part of the summer holiday, with the older youth fellowship members acting as leaders. Then there is a summer weekend event for teenagers. This is also run by the senior youth fellowship members. The young leaders themselves are encouraged to attend Christian young people's holidays arranged by national groups, such as the CYFA Holidays and the Greenbelt Festival. Another source of encouragement and instruction for young people takes place in the context of the annual parish weekend.

As well as being so involved with children and young people through his own church, the Revd Kenneth Bates tries to make frequent and widespread contact with children and young people in other ways outside the church. He is a frequent visitor to the local brownies, cubs, guides and scouts. He is often to be found making informal visits to the parish's local education authority primary school, and from time to time he travels out to visit the neighbouring secondary school. Occasionally he is invited to take an assembly in the local primary school, or to take a lesson in the local secondary school. He also co-operates with the other denomination which is involved in youth work in the parish, and he encourages members of his congregation to become involved in local secular youth work.

The commitment of Long Barland church to a ministry among young people is carried right through to the membership of the parochial church council. At present, there are 3 young people under the age of twenty-two who serve as elected members of the parochial church council. In this way, Long Barland church is enabling young people to take a full part in the decisions affecting the life of their parish church, and to have a real share in the responsibility for their church's future. Long Barland is a good place to end our drive round some of the varied parishes in a rural Anglican diocese. Long Barland gives us some real hope for the future, and a vision of what is still possible, given the energy, the faith and the resources.

11 A DEANERY IN DEPTH

The previous seven chapters have provided us with a detailed picture of rural Anglicanism today – as seen through the eyes of the clergymen who work in a rural diocese. I did not wish to leave the story there. It is one thing to know how the situation looks to those on the inside who are responsible for running the rural churches, but how does it look to those on the outside? For example, what impression is the visitor likely to receive of the rural Anglican church if he or she were suddenly to decide to attend a Sunday service?

This kind of question requires a completely different kind of research project. My opportunity came when a group of ordinands decided to set aside one of their weekends in order to work as my volunteer research assistants. We decided to select just one deanery and to make a detailed study of that deanery in depth. Our aim was to visit every church in the deanery on the Saturday in order to have a look around, and then to return on the Sunday to attend all the Sunday church services. We chose the third Sunday in May.

In order to be systematic and thorough in our research, we spent a lot of time preparing ourselves before setting out. As a group we worked out what we wanted to learn about the churches and about the Sunday services. Then each ordinand set out with a detailed research schedule to complete in order to collect objective information and to record accurately their reactions.

We selected a deanery from the *Diocesan Year Book*. There were twenty-one parishes in this deanery, each with its own parish church. Fifteen of the parishes were small villages of under 400 inhabitants, another five of them were villages ranging between 500 and 2,000 inhabitants, and there was also a town of over 16,000 inhabitants. According to the *Diocesan Year Book*, these parishes were staffed by thirteen clergymen, including an assistant curate, a retired clergyman, a non-stipendiary minister and two clergy who were also serving parishes in neighbouring deaneries. Armed with this information and an ordinance survey map, the group set out on the Saturday to visit each of the twenty-one churches.

The first impression given by the majority of the churches in the deanery was that a great deal of care and attention was generally being invested in their maintenance and upkeep. Seventeen of the twenty-one churches looked well cared for and loved: the churchyard grass was under control and the buildings themselves did not look neglected. The other four churches presented a sadder picture, with overgrown churchyards and neglected buildings.

Having arrived, the visitors tried the door latch to see if they could get into the church. Eight of the twenty-one churches were kept open and the visitors could walk straight in. Another seven were locked, but the name and the address of the key-holder was given. Some of the addresses were easy to find, while others, like 'Mrs Goodenough, Loveday's Cottage' were of more help to the locals than to the visitors, especially when it was discovered that Mrs Goodenough had left the village some months earlier and that 'Loveday's Cottage' had apparently never carried a name board.

The other six churches, which were locked and gave no indication of where the key could be obtained, presented a much greater challenge to the visitor. The assumption is obviously made that neither residents nor strangers use these village churches as a place for prayer or reflection. They have become museums, locked to preserve the treasures of a past generation.

Especially in those situations in which the village rectory has been closed, the church building often acts as the main and only point of proclamation between the church and the rural community. How much use does the rural church make of its buildings as a way of drawing attention to the life of the local worshipping community? If visitors approach the church building, can they find the information that they need in order to seek the help of the clergy or to discover the times of Sunday services?

Our team of ordinands discovered that just half of the churches displayed some information about the local vicar. Ten churches gave his name, while nine of them also gave an address and eight gave a telephone number. Eleven of the twenty-one churches gave no information about the vicar. If rural Anglican churches are reticent about how to contact the local clergy, they are even more reticent about how to contact the churchwardens. Only five of the twenty-one churches displayed the churchwardens' names, while only two of them also gave their addresses.

Sunday services were clearly advertised at sixteen of the twenty-one churches. The other five churches presented the visitor with something of a problem. Since they wanted to come back to a service on the following day, the only way they could discover the time of the service was by obtaining the vicar's name from the *Diocesan Year Book* and by telephoning him. This worked in the case of four of the five churches, but failed in the other case, since not even the *Diocesan Year Book* contained the clergyman's address and telephone number.

Four of the churches we visited on the Saturday were not holding a service on the following Sunday, and we were unable to discover whether another one of them was holding a service or not. In the remaining sixteen churches there was a total of twenty-four services on the Sunday. Twelve of the churches had just one service, while the other four had three services each. Our day, then, involved attending six early morning Holy Communion services: four at 8.00 a.m., one at 8.30 a.m. and one at 9.00 a.m.; seven mid-morning or late morning Communion services: four at 10.00 a.m., two at 10.30 a.m. and one at 11.15 a.m; four services of Matins: one at 10.00 a.m., two at 11.00 a.m. and one at 11.15 a.m; one Family Service at 10.30 a.m; and six Evensongs: two at 3.00 p.m., one at 3.30 p.m. and three at 6.30 p.m. Just one or two of our group attended each service.

When strangers walk into a church, the first thing that they notice is the kind of welcome they are given. The ordinands tried to arrive at each of the services so that they could be there about five minutes before the service was due to start. At eight of the twenty-four services there was no-one waiting to greet them as they arrived. They had to discover for themselves which books they needed in order to be able to follow the service, and to find themselves a seat. At three of the services the clergyman was waiting by the door to welcome the congregation, and at another thirteen there were lay people handing out the books. At just six of the twenty-four services the visitor was shown to a seat.

While the visitors were waiting for the service to begin, they counted the congregations. At the majority of the services this was not an arduous task. Six of the twenty-four services were attended by a congregation of 5 or less, while a further nine had between 6 and 10 people in the congregation. Another three services had a congregation of between 11 and 20 people. This means that just six of the services were attended by a congregation of more than 20 people. Four of these better attended services were mid-morning Communions, one was a Matins and the other an evening Evensong.

Generally the congregations counted by the visitors were smaller than those estimated by the clergymen in the diocesan census reported in the earlier chapters. Throughout the whole of the deanery, the clergymen's estimate of their Sunday church attendance was 40%

higher than the number of people actually counted by the visitors. The total number of people counted at the twenty-four services was 394, which represents 1.5% of the population of the deanery.

Waiting for the services to begin, the visitors were able to study the members of the congregation in greater depth. To begin with, they worked out the proportions of men and women attending these churches. They discovered that two-thirds (67%) of the total number of church attenders were women, and just one-third (33%) were men. This ratio was roughly consistent for the different types of services and for the different times of day.

Next, the visitors looked at the age of the people who attended church. Of the 394 people counted in the congregations, 70 were children and young people under the age of twenty-two and the other 324 were adults over the age of twenty-one. It is interesting to look at the adult church attenders first. Four out of every seven of the 324 adults (57%) were over the age of sixty, while the majority of the others were between the ages of forty and sixty. There were in fact very few young adults between the ages of twenty-two and forty attending church in the deanery. Looked at another way, two out of every five of the services (42%) had no-one in the congregation under forty years of age.

The 70 children and young people who came to church on that Sunday from the twenty-one parishes were to be found at eight of the twenty-four services. The other sixteen services had no children or young people in the congregation at all. The eight services which had some children and young people present were two early Holy Communion services, four mid-morning Holy Communion services, one mid-morning Matins and one evening Evensong. At three of these services there was just one young worshipper, while at another there were just two worshippers under the age of twenty-two. The other four services had in fact 9, 11, 21 and 24 young people each.

Looking more closely at the age of these children and young people, over half are aged between six and thirteen. There are only 11 children under the age of six at services in this deanery, and 21 between the ages of fourteen and twenty-one. This parallels the pattern evident in the larger diocesan survey. In addition to the Sunday services, four of the twenty-one parishes in the deanery run a Sunday school for children. Two of these Sunday schools are run concurrently with the mid-morning Communion service. In both cases, the children are present for part of the service in church and so were counted by the visitors as part of the church congregation. One of the other two Sunday schools was held on alternate Sundays when there was no Family Communion service in the parish church, and the fourth is held in church at 2.30 p.m. on Sunday afternoon.

Since the majority of the congregations are small, the visitors felt that their presence could not go unnoticed, either by the clergymen or by the regular attenders. When the minister sees a visitor in the small congregation of a rural Anglican church, does he try to offer any help in guiding the congregation through the service, or does he assume that the visitors, like everyone else in the congregation, know their way around the Church of England services? The visitors discovered that at the majority of the services, no help was given to enable strangers to find their place in the service book.

During the services, the visitors paid particular attention to four things, the number of lay people involved in the service in one way or another, the music, the sermon and their own personal comfort.

As far as the visitors could see, the main involvement of lay people in the twenty-four services in the deanery was in giving out books at the beginning of the service and taking the collection during the service. Lay people were giving out the books at thirteen of the twenty-four services. Generally just one lay person was employed in this way; although at four of the services they were working in pairs. Collections were taken during the service at seventeen of the twenty-four services. Again, usually only one person was needed to pass the plate around, although at four of the services the collectors were working in pairs. Giving out the books and taking the collection seem to be tasks reserved for the senior members of the rural Anglican churches. At none of the services were either of these jobs undertaken by anyone under the age of twenty-two.

At thirteen of the twenty-four services, the clergymen conducted the whole of the worship themselves from beginning to end, while at the majority of the other services lay participation in leadership was kept to a minimum. At eleven of the services lay people took part as lesson readers. However, in all except two of the services, either the same lay person read both lessons or the clergyman read one of them. It was very rare to involve two different lay people as lesson readers in the same service. Another interesting observation is that no children or young people under the age of twenty-two were involved as lesson readers. Again, this is a privilege reserved for the senior members of the congregation.

Some of the Communion services also involved lay people as altar servers or as members of a procession to bring the bread and the wine to the altar. The offertory processions were again always composed of adults, while most of the servers were children.

Music plays an important part in worship. Hymns and psalms are often thought of as an essential component of a church service. The problem is that small rural churches often have insufficient people in their congregations to make singing at all comfortable. The visitors found that nineteen of the twenty-four services included hymns. At eighteen of these services the hymns were accompanied by an organ or a harmonium, sometimes very badly played. At the other service, where there was only one other person in the congregation apart from the visitor, the vicar tried to lead unaccompanied singing.

Generally the visitors felt that the congregational singing was poor and unenthusiastic. The visitors also felt uneasy about joining in, feeling conspicuous or embarrassed if their voices should begin to sound above those of the more regular worshippers. There was a choir at seven of the services, but only in the case of three were they judged as actually helping the singing.

The sermon is the central means of teaching in the rural Anglican church today, but by no means all services include a sermon. In fact, a sermon was preached at sixteen of the twenty-four services in the deanery on that Sunday. Generally, the visitors were not impressed by the standard of preaching. Six of the sermons were rated as interesting, while the other ten were considered dull or boring. The biggest complaint was that somehow many of the sermons failed to be relevant either to the rest of the service or to the real issues of life. Preaching to small congregations can be a difficult and disheartening task, and the majority of the clergy in the deanery were regarded by the ordinands to have given up really trying.

Church services involve quite a lot of sitting and kneeling, but somehow the majority of church pews seem to have been designed without much understanding of the human shape. After being in church for the whole of the service, many of the visitors came away saying that the seats had been very uncomfortable. In fact, only two of the sixteen churches visited that day were comfortable to sit in. While I am sure that it can be argued that people should not go to church to be comfortable, very little can be gained by furnishing churches with pews that positively add to the worshippers' discomfort.

When the service was finished, the visitors wondered whether either the clergyman or any of the congregation would talk with them. After fourteen of the twenty-four services someone from the congregation spoke to the visitors. At the other ten services, all the regular worshippers completely ignored the stranger in their midst. After eighteen of the services, the minister made a point of speaking to the visitors. Fifteen of the visitors felt that the minister was showing a friendly welcome to them; the other three felt that they were being cross-examined about their unexpected attendance at the service. At the other six services, the visitors were surprised that the clergymen made no attempt to speak to them either before the service or after it. They felt that this complete lack of personal contact was unlikely to encourage them to return to that church again, even if they lived locally.

Finally, before leaving the church the visitors looked round to see how well equipped the churches were with book stalls, display screens, notice boards and the like. There was a book stall in just five of the sixteen churches, and only one of them looked attractive and well stocked. The others were untidy and displayed faded and obsolete books. There was a display screen in just four of the sixteen churches. Again, only one of them was put to attractive use, while the others were described as shabby. Surprisingly enough, five of the sixteen churches did not have a notice board of any sort. Moreover, of the eleven churches where a notice board was in evidence, six were said to be in poor condition, and none was thought to be really well used. Shabby, out of date or unimaginative notices do not reflect a lively Christian community.

When the late comers had returned from the last Evensongs of that Sunday, the group of ordinands sat round and reflected on their weekend's work. They were both a lot wiser and a good deal sadder for their experience.

12 ATTENDING SERVICES – the visitor's view

The previous chapter has given us an overall impression of what was found by the group of ordinands and their friends when they set out on the third Sunday in May to attend all the twenty-four church services conducted in a rural Anglican deanery. The experience made a lasting impression on them. It is well worth our while, therefore, to try to enter more fully into the events of their day. In this chapter, we will join some of the group as they attend their chosen service.

There is insufficient space in this chapter to describe all twenty-four services, so we must be content with a selection. The nine services we shall attend alongside the ordinands begin with two early morning Holy Communion services, one in a village of about 1,000 inhabitants and the other in a village of 200 inhabitants. Then we move on to three mid-morning Holy Communion services in communities varying from 1,200 to 2,200 inhabitants. Sunday morning will finish with two late morning services, a Matins in a village of 100 inhabitants and a surprise service, advertised as a Communion on the notice board but in fact appearing as something quite different, in a village of nearly 200 inhabitants. Later in the day we will visit two Evensongs, one during the afternoon at 3.30 p.m. in a village of about 700 inhabitants and the other at 6.30 p.m. in the one town in the deanery of 16,000 inhabitants. The names attributed to these parishes are, once again, fictitious but the descriptions are factual, based on the visitors' careful observation and documentation of their visits.

8.00 a.m. Holy Communion

Stephen got up early to drive out to Sutton Green to arrive in time for the 8 o'clock celebration of Holy Communion. Sutton Green is one of the show places of the county, and is often featured in countryside magazines and picture calendars. The fourteenth century church tower rises majestically behind the picturesque village green and the thatched cottages.

Stephen found the whole setting most inspiring as he parked his car some way from the church and walked across the village green, bathed in the early light of a fine May morning. As he walked through the lychgate, Stephen was impressed by the care obviously lavished on the churchyard and on the church itself. As he entered the porch, his eye was caught by the notice board, where well designed up-to-date notices gave him a good idea of church life in Sutton Green.

Sutton Green has a population of about 1,000, and a church electoral roll of over 150 names. The church here had a parson all to itself until a few years ago when it was required to share its incumbent with a small village five miles away. On most Sundays, however, Sutton Green is still able, with the help of a reader, to maintain its traditional pattern of an early morning Holy Communion, a mid-morning Matins or Parish Communion on alternate Sundays, and an Evensong. Thus, Stephen was attending the first of the three services to be held here in the course of the day.

It was now five minutes to eight and Stephen wondered what he would find when he opened the door and walked in. He was greeted by an elderly lady who gave him a prayer book. Apart from this one lady, the church was completely empty. He reckoned that the church was capable of seating upwards of 200 people. He chose a pew near the back and sat down. Even the pew felt as if it would be comfortable. He took the beautiful hand-made tapestry kneeler from its hook and thought of the people who had so recently given of their time to make it.

A couple of minutes to eight the rest of the congregation arrived. They came in silently and scattered themselves in odd pews throughout the church. Besides himself, there were 4 men and 7 women attending the service. They were all over fifty. Seven of them were sitting alone, while the other four sat in two pairs. Stephen thought that they looked so lonely and lost in such a large church.

On the dot of 8 o'clock, the rector processed in from the vestry, wearing a surplice and stole. He was a man in his mid-sixties. The service was traditional and formal, following the order of the 1662 *Book of Common Prayer*. There were no hymns and no sermon. The congregation was obviously very familiar with the order of service and no help was given to a visitor who might have been unfamiliar with it. Stephen wondered how he would have managed to follow the service if he had been a total stranger, not only to Sutton Green but to the whole of the Anglican Church.

Stephen felt that the rector conducted the service with a sense of dignity and involvement, although it all seemed a little impersonal and removed. He conducted the whole of the service from the main altar at the far end of the large chancel, while the congregation was scattered towards the back of the nave. The only lay participation in the service was when the lady who had given Stephen his prayer book also took the collection. The rector read both of the lessons himself.

The service lasted 32 minutes. When it was all over, Stephen got up to go. The congregation drifted away as silently and as suddenly as it had appeared. The lady who had given him his prayer book when he arrived stood by the door to make sure that he gave it up as he left. He said good morning and walked out into the churchyard again. The rector remained in the vestry and made no personal contact with his congregation either before or after the service. As a visitor, Stephen went away feeling strangely empty. He had shared the early morning meal with the people of God, but had somehow failed to meet them. And he wondered how the other worshippers were feeling as they made their way home to breakfast. Were they going back to eat breakfast alone, going back to empty houses and to empty lives? He rather feared that they were.

8.30 a.m. Holy Communion

Sally made a slightly later start than Stephen, and set out to attend the 8.30 a.m. Holy Communion service at Great Washbrook. She knew that Great Washbrook was part of a three parish benefice, with Little Washbrook and Little Debly. The early morning Holy Communion was to be the only service in Great Washbrook on that Sunday. As she made her way through the roughly mown churchyard and along the overgrown church path, she wondered how many of the 250 inhabitants of Great Washbrook would be joining her at the early morning service.

Great Washbrook church is entered from the north side. In spite of the brightness of the morning, the north porch looked dull and uninviting. There were no notices in the porch at all. The large church door creaked as she pushed it open. In the church there were 2 elderly ladies, both sitting in the far aisle, but some distance from each other. There was no one to greet Sally as she arrived, so she helped herself to a prayer book and chose somewhere inconspicuous to sit. A minute or two later the door creaked again and 2 other elderly ladies walked in. They sat together in an area of the church away from those who had arrived before them. The congregation was now complete – 4 ladies, all over the age of sixty in a church large enough to seat about 180 people. Shortly after half-past eight the sixty year old parish priest hurried in from the vestry at the back of the church and took up his place at the altar. It was the 1662 *Book of Common Prayer* Communion service, without hymns, sermon or notices. The vicar read both lessons himself.

The only participation from the congregation was when one of the ladies took the collection bag round to the others in the church.

The impression that stuck in Sally's mind most about the service was the speed with which it was conducted. She felt that the priest rushed through the service very quickly and rather carelessly. The whole service was over in seventeen minutes. Sally said that she couldn't help noticing how scruffy the priest looked. He was wearing a grubby and crumpled surplice, and a lot of the time he had both hands in his cassock pockets, with the surplice bunched up over them. She felt that the priest was not really interested in what he was doing.

After the service, Sally looked round the church. She said that the church felt rather sad, musty and uncared for, although there were some very nice flowers on the altar. She could see no signs of a parish magazine, a notice board or a bookstall, or any other source of information about the life and the work of the church in the parish. While she was looking round, the vicar came up to her. After seeing the way in which he had conducted the service and ignored the other members of the congregation as they went out, it took her greatly by surprise to discover how friendly and approachable he was. They talked together for some time about the church. The four ladies in the congregation slipped away without speaking to her.

10.00 a.m. Parish Communion

Nick chose to attend a mid-morning Parish Communion service in Sparham, a village of just over 1,000 inhabitants. He arrived at Sparham in good time and walked round the outside of the church. This is a fine building, built in the decorated style of around 1320. Nick was especially impressed by the fine chancel, with the extravagant tracery of the large east window.

When he had finished admiring the building, Nick entered the porch and pushed open the large wooden door. A lay person was waiting just inside the door, ready to welcome him and to give him two books, a Series 3 Communion pamphlet and a copy of *Hymns Ancient and Modern Revised*. Nick was left to find his own way to a seat. One of the guide books to the churches of the county describes the pews in Sparham church as belonging to the seventeenth century and being 'of an unusual shape'. Nick had not been sitting in the church for many minutes before he realised that whatever were the historic or aesthetic merits of the pews, they had certainly never been designed for comfort.

Looking round the inside of the church, Nick felt that the whole building looked well cared for and loved. The church was clean looking and the flowers were fresh and artistically arranged. The hymn book and service book were quite new and in good condition. The kneelers were smart and of a sensible design. At the back of the church, there was both a display screen and bookstall; both seemed to be fairly well used, if not particularly attractive in their arrangement.

While he was sitting there, Nick observed the rest of the congregation come in. By 10 o'clock there were 23 people in church. Although the church could seat about 180, these 23 worshippers did not really look lost in a large building, as can so often happen. They tended to sit together and towards the front, with only two of them sitting alone and looking out on a limb. Looking more closely at his fellow worshippers, Nick realised that there were three times as many women as men in the congregation: there were 6 men and 17 women. He also realised that the majority of the congregation was quite elderly. Fifteen of the 23 worshippers were clearly over the age of sixty, and, apart from the one teenager, the others were all in their forties or fifties. There were no young adults in the congregation at all and only the one young person.

As the clock struck 10, Nick was beginning to wonder why he had seen no signs of the vicar. Then, suddenly, the church door burst open and the vicar came rushing in. Nick says that the vicar then 'flew round the church putting things out'. The problem is that the vicar of Sparham has two other churches in his care and that morning he had already celebrated Communion in them both, at 8.00 a.m. and 9.00 a.m.

Before the vicar had arrived, Nick had felt that there was an atmosphere of quiet prayer in the church, an appropriate preparation for worship. All this was rudely destroyed as the vicar tried to organise himself for the service. Nick felt sorry for the congregation; he felt even sorrier for the parish priest who had allowed himself to get pushed into such a tight schedule. Nick began to wonder whether it really was helpful for a parish priest to celebrate Communion at 8.00 a.m., 9.00 a.m. and 10.00 a.m. in three different churches, and, if this was inevitable, whether it would be possible to encourage greater lay participation in preparing the churches before the priest arrived.

The service began just seven minutes late. The vicar set off at a breathless pace, and none of the congregation could keep up. Consequently, the congregation took very little active part in the service and only joined in the prayers with a half-hearted mumble. They seemed to have become accustomed to being treated as spectators rather than as participants and so no longer really tried to participate.

The brisk pace of the service meant that it was all over in forty-eight minutes.

Four hymns were sung in the course of the service. Nick found these particularly painful. The organist was slow and far from accurate in selecting the right notes. There was no choir to help lead the singing, and the vicar felt that it was his responsibility to give a loud lead. In fact, he paid little attention to the speed of the organ or indeed to the words in the hymn book. The congregation preferred to listen to this battle between the organist and the vicar, without themselves taking sides. Nick felt this to be a particular shame since the hymns had been well chosen and he would have liked to have been able to join in singing them. The service began with 'Thou art the way: by thee alone from sin and death we flee'. The gradual hymn was 'Lord, in thy name thy servants plead, And thou hast sworn to hear' to Ravenscroft's well known tune 'Lincoln'. For the offertory they had the communion hymn 'I hunger and I thirst', and the service closed with one of Nick's favourite hymns 'For the beauty of the earth'.

The sermon was a strange experience. The vicar spoke loudly and forcefully for nine minutes, but very quickly lost the attention of his congregation. No use was made of visual aids or anecdotes to stimulate attention or to elicit response. Nick was unable to find a theme or thread running through the sermon. The whole style was didactic and forceful. Authoritative and controversial statements seem to have been made without any support of logic, argument or fact.

The form of service was slightly high church. The vicar wore vestments and was assisted by the teenage boy in the congregation acting as an altar server. Five of the other people in the congregation took some small part in the service. One man was giving out books before the service began, a man and a woman took the collection, and another couple brought the bread and the wine to the altar. All of these five people who took an active part in the service were in their sixties or seventies. At Sparham church lay people were not encouraged to read lessons.

After the service, the vicar stood by the door as the congregation went out and he tried to speak to each one of them. However, there was something cold and uncaring in his attitude. When it came to Nick's turn, the vicar shook him by the hand and said that he would be always welcome to come again. Nick replied that he was just passing through. The vicar was not listening. 'No matter; you'll always be welcome', he repeated. Nick agreed that it didn't really seem to matter at all.

10.00 a.m. Parish Eucharist

Terry elected to visit Kessing Baston. During the past twenty years, Kessing Baston has grown from a small straggling village to a community of just over 2,000 inhabitants. Several new estates have been built and a large number of newcomers have settled into the area.

Kessing Baston church is not much to look at from the outside, but inside it is one of the ecclesiastical curiosities of the diocese. The church has retained its box pews, dominated by an uncommonly complete Jacobean three-decker pulpit, including a tester and hour-glass stand. Every inch of the nave is tightly fitted with the box pews, elevated family pews for the local squirearchy of a past age, and ranks of elevated pews for children at the west end of the aisles, complete with a special boxed-in seat for the schoolmaster and schoolmistress to watch the children. Above the pews, the walls are rich with panelling, faded painting and a wide range of memorials and monuments.

The floor of the south porch of Kessing Baston church is built several feet higher than the floor of the nave. Terry did not know about this difference in the height of the two floors. He pushed open the door and fell down the step to make quite a dramatic entrance into the church. Both the vicar and the churchwarden were standing just inside the door ready to welcome the congregation. They put out a hand to help Terry steady himself, made him feel welcome and assured him that he was not the first visitor to be caught out by the step. Terry wondered why they did nothing to make the entrance to their church a little safer for the unwary.

Terry let himself into one of the ancient box pews and peered out at the rest of the congregation who seemed to be peering out of their boxes at·him. He wondered how on earth a building furnished like this and so obviously designed for the church's needs in an earlier age could ever bring worship to life in the 1980s.

As he came in, Terry had been given a hymn book and a service book. The hymn book was a tatty copy of the *English Hymnal* and the service book was one which he had never met before. Kessing Baston church used neither the *Book of Common Prayer* nor the recent forms of service developed by the Church of England as a whole, but a Mass booklet produced by an independent church press. Terry realised that he had arrived in a high church parish.

Although Kessing Baston church looked like a museum, the congregation itself was far from geriatric. What made this congregation so different from any others in the deanery was the fact that instead of the over-sixties predominating, they were noticeable by their very absence. Out of a total congregation of 30 people, there were 6 toddlers under the age of six, 4 children between six and thirteen years of age, 3 young people between fourteen and twenty-one and 3 adults under the age of forty. Ten other members of the congregation were in their forties and fifties, and only 4 were over the age of sixty. In addition to the 30 people in the congregation, there were 11 others forming a choir, including 3 adults and 8 children and young people. There were also 2 eight year old boys assisting in the service as altar servers.

Thus, over half of those attending the service were under the age of twenty-one. Moreover, the notices indicated that a Sunday school was taking place somewhere else in the village at the same time as the morning service. Here indeed, thought Terry, was a rural Anglican church trying to do its work among young people.

The vicar of Kessing Baston has care for just the one parish church, but is also chaplain to a neighbouring hospital. On a Sunday morning, he conducts an 8.00 a.m. Communion service in his parish church, a 9.00 a.m. Communion in the hospital and then returns to his church for the 10.00 a.m. Parish Eucharist, which is the main service of the day. Evensong takes place in the parish church at 3.00 p.m.

The vicar was so busy making people welcome and talking to them before the service that the service itself started five minutes late. It then lasted for fifty-five minutes. Terry felt that the service itself was a strange mixture of the friendly and the formal, the relaxed and the high church. The priest was obviously working hard to overcome the difficulties created by the way in which his church was designed and furnished. A sense of sincerity and involvement came through in the way in which he conducted the service, but Terry felt that it must have been a long time since the parish priest last sat in the congregation and actually experienced a service in the same way as the congregation experienced it. It was all rather rushed, and somehow the priest seemed to be dragging the congregation along in such a way that they had to struggle to keep up. He gave them insufficient time to find their places in the book, to stand, to sit or to kneel before a new stage in the service was undertaken. He led the prayers just a little too quickly, so that the congregation had difficulty in synchronising with his timing. In spite of this, the congregation was doing its best to participate. The congregational responses were good and clear, and, once he had become accustomed to the pace, Terry found himself both wanting and being able to join in.

Terry was impressed by the way in which quite a range of the laity took some active role in the service. As well as the part played by the eleven people in the choir and the two altar servers, ten of the thirty people in the congregation had some special job to do. Two ladies in their sixties were giving out books before the service began. Two men in their forties took the collection. Two other men in their forties and a six year old boy carried the bread, water and wine to the altar. One layman read a lesson, and another led the intercessions. A layman came out of the congregation to administer the chalice.

All told, Terry felt that Kessing Baston church was doing a good job, but he also made three interesting criticisms. He felt that as a visitor it would have been very helpful if someone had given some guidance with the order of service, especially since Kessing Baston church was using a book with which visitors were unlikely to be familiar. He felt that it was a pity that no opportunity was taken at the peace for the congregation to greet each other and to make the visitor feel more at home. Finally, he was disappointed that two of the four hymns used in the service were taken from a book which only the choir possessed and not the congregation. The choir were using *With Cheerful Voice*, the hymn book used in the village school. Two hymns were especially chosen because they were known to the children, 'Father, lead me day by day Ever in thine own sweet way', and 'All things which live below the sky'. Terry thought that the idea of building bridges between the hymns used in school and those used in church was an excellent one, but that it fell flat when even the children in the congregation were unable to join in because of a lack of books.

After the service, the vicar was standing by the door, speaking to people as they left. He made a particular point of catching Terry by the arm as someone who had not been to Kessing Baston church before. Terry explained that he was just visiting, but the vicar was not content with such a simple answer: he wanted full details of name and address. Instead of being made to feel welcome, Terry suddenly felt under great pressure. He realised that the parish priest had to tread a delicate line between making the visitor feel welcome and not invading his privacy; and on this occasion he felt that the line was not being observed. For this reason alone, Terry would be reluctant, if he lived in the area, to return to Kessing Baston church again in a hurry.

10.30 a.m. Family Communion

Martin's choice was to visit Perrett, a small market town of about 2,000 inhabitants. Perrett must have been a prosperous community in the middle ages, overshadowed by a Norman castle and a thirteenth century monastery. The massive parish church is the last surviving monument to Perrett's medieval grandeur. It is the kind of building which could easily seat 400 people. Now Perrett shares its vicar with a neighbouring village and is reduced to a pattern of one regular service each Sunday morning, and an evening service on alternate Sundays.

When Martin arrived at the church in time for the 10.30 a.m. Family Communion service, he was given a handful of books by a middle-aged sidesman. There was no sign of welcome on the sidesman's face, and no words passed between them. Martin sat down and looked through the books he had been given. There was a Series 3 Communion booklet, a copy of the *English Hymnal*, a fat blue book which contained both the *Book of Common Prayer* and the *Standard Edition of Hymns Ancient and Modern*, and a copy of *100 Hymns for Today*. He tried placing them all on the pew ledge in front of him, but the pile was too big and they toppled off. He looked at the numbers on the hymn board and couldn't make up his mind to which of the three hymn books they referred.

There were already quite a few people in church when Martin arrived, and he watched the rest of the congregation gradually assemble. By the time the service was ready to start, there were 37 people in the congregation, 27 of whom were female and 10 male. About half of the congregation were over the age of sixty. There were also 9 between the ages of forty and sixty, 7 adults under the age of forty, and 3 children.

The service began five minutes late. The choir and vicar processed in while singing the first hymn. The choir was made up by 8 children between the ages of six and thirteen, and 4 adults. As the service was beginning in church, the Sunday school was beginning in the vicarage next door. The idea is that the Sunday school joins the main church service at the offertory. This week there were 20 children in the Sunday school and 3 adults working with them. Thus, by the end of the service, there were 31 children and young people and 41 adults in church.

Martin thought that it was a good idea to have the Sunday school involved in the main Sunday morning service, but in practice he saw that this method of working carried with it certain difficulties that Perrett church had failed to overcome. First, there is the problem of timing. How does the Sunday school know when to come across to church? This week they mis-timed their arrival badly and had to wait in the porch for five or six minutes before they could come in. The children chattered and shuffled while the intercessions were dragging on in the service, and it felt to Martin as if the congregation's whole attention was concentrated not on the praying inside the church but on the children outside.

The next problem is to know how to integrate the children into the service after they have arrived. Again, Perrett church failed badly. Far from either the priest or the congregation welcoming the children as they entered, the idea seemed to be to try to pretend that the children were not coming to join the service at all. The children came in during a hymn: during the same hymn the collection was taken and the offertory procession was formed. The congregation was far too busy singing or looking for their collection money to notice the children. The children had to collect a set of hymn books and somehow find out which hymn was being sung. Instead of being dispersed among the congregation, the children were filed into two rows near the back. In this situation the Sunday school teachers were unable to help the children find their places in the books. At the same time, the children were unable to see what was taking place at the altar, where the rest of the service was conducted, at the far East end of the chancel. From the very start the children fidgeted and looked bored. Martin felt sorry for them.

Although quite a lot of children were at this service, no attempt was made to catch their interest, or to involve them actively in any way. The lesson readers, the sidesmen and those taking part in the offertory procession were all over the age of fifty. The children and young people were able to offer nothing of their own to the service.

As a visitor, Martin says that he experienced great difficulty in feeling at home or comfortable in this service. To Martin, the service felt far too impersonal and formal, treating him as a spectator rather than as a participant. He also felt that there was far too much singing in the service. All told, there were seven hymns and a psalm, and some of the hymns were lengthy ones, like the six eight-line verses of 'O Worship the King'. The choir and organist were in good form, but for some reason the congregation never really joined in the singing and Martin felt inhibited about enjoying singing himself when those around him were hardly singing at all. The problem is that the sheer size of the building makes congregational singing difficult, especially when the congregation are scattered throughout the nave and the choir concentrated some distance away in the chancel.

The sermon was on the theme of Rogationtide. It lasted for twelve minutes and Martin gave a silent sigh of relief when it was ended.

The service itself ended at 11.43 a.m. While people were beginning to make their way out, Martin decided to look round the church. In one of the aisles there was a bookstall which seemed to carry a good supply of up-to-date literature. The stall seemed well set out, but Martin could not actually look at any of the books because the whole stall was covered by a heavy transparent plastic sheet. The intention was apparently to keep the books clean: it also seemed to keep them unsold and unread. In another aisle there was a display screen, but this was unattractive and seemed to have little to proclaim. While Martin was looking round the church, one or two people from the congregation smiled at him and spoke to him. He appreciated the human contact with the other worshippers.

Eventually Martin joined the queue waiting to go through the door. The queue was moving very slowly because the vicar was trying to speak to everyone in turn. When it came to Martin's turn he felt that he was being cross-examined about who he was, where he came from and what he was doing. Martin would have been happy to stop and talk, but he felt embarrassed about the people behind him who were still waiting to escape from the church. Consequently, Martin tried to get through the vicar's questions as quickly as possible and make his way back to the car.

11.15 a.m. Matins

Stanston church is a fine example of the late fifteenth century perpendicular style added to an earlier tower. The church here serves a small village of less than 100 inhabitants. It shares its parish priest with three other larger villages. On the third Sunday in the month, the rector of Stanston has already conducted an 8.00 a.m. Holy Communion and a 10.00 a.m. Matins, before travelling on to Stanston to conduct his third service of the morning, Matins at 11.15 a.m.

Richard chose to experience Matins at Stanston. He arrived at the church in good time and was greeted in a most friendly way by the churchwarden. The churchwarden introduced himself as Lieutenant-Colonel Danby-Smith and explained that his family had been the patrons of Stanston church for generations. He also pointed out to Richard some of the more interesting memorials in the church to the Danby-Smith family.

When Richard had chosen a pew, he discovered that there was a prayer book and a hymn book already there. These were the *Book of Common Prayer* and *Hymns Ancient and Modern Revised*. It seemed to Richard as if the prayer book had been sitting in the pew for years. The psalms were numbered in roman numerals and the prayer for the royal family prayed for 'Our gracious Queen Mary, Alexandra the Queen

Mother and Edward, Prince of Wales'. Apart from Richard and Lieutenant-Colonel Danby-Smith, there were 3 elderly ladies in the congregation and 2 other elderly ladies sitting in a family pew in the chancel, behind the vicar's stall. Richard watched these two ladies walk in through their own private door in the chancel. Throughout the service they kept a close watch on the congregation, but made no personal contact with any of them. After the service they slipped out by the same door as they had entered.

The vicar arrived precisely at 11.15 a.m. and spent five minutes or so trying to light a calor gas stove near his stall. The stove went out again during the first hymn and the vicar had another attempt at lighting it.

The service was formal prayerbook Matins. The Venite, Te Deum and Jubilate were all sung, together with the psalm set for the day. There were also three hymns. The service began just after 11.20 a.m. with 'New every morning is the love'. The collection was taken during 'God of mercy, God of grace' and the service ended with 'Thy kingdom come O God'. The elderly lady organist had particular difficulty with the psalm and, with such a small congregation, even the hymns did not go at all well. Richard describes the whole exercise as 'disastrous and pointless; we all tried to sing, but none of us really could'.

The vicar preached a fifteen minute sermon. He faced his congregation of five from the pulpit, while the organist and the two ladies in the family pew remained firmly out of sight. Richard thought that it must be quite disheartening to preach to such a small congregation, and he was not surprised that the preacher seemed to be putting so little effort into what he was doing. Richard says 'the sermon did not seem carefully put together: the priest had a written text but made little use of it'. As far as Richard could judge, no-one seemed to be listening to the sermon anyway.

There was no lay participation in the service as the vicar read both lessons and read all the prayers. Richard felt this was a pity, especially since the vicar had not had time to prepare the service beforehand. He was looking up the lessons and reading through them during the canticles and psalm, and he was selecting the prayers during the hymns. On top of all this, the vicar was continually distracted by checking whether the calor gas stove was still burning or whether it had gone out again.

The service finished at 12.10 p.m. The vicar was standing at the door to greet people as they went out. He shook Richard warmly by the hand and gave him a friendly smile. In spite of it all, Richard was pleased that he had met the man and he felt that he would like to get to know him better.

11.15 a.m. Special Service

Phillip decided to attend the late morning service at Great Wraggington, a small village of about 160 inhabitants. Great Wraggington is one of those rural churches which do not consider it necessary to display any information about themselves. There is no notice board in the porch, no indication of the incumbent's name and address, no list of services, no indication of where to obtain the key. However, on the lychgate there was a faded list of the pattern of Sunday services. The list had been written with a ballpoint pen and although the colour of the ink had now disappeared, it was still possible to read the indentation made on the paper by the ballpoint itself. On his way through the lychgate, Phillip checked that on the third Sunday in the month the service was Holy Communion at 11.15 a.m.

Looking more carefully at the list, Phillip realised how important it was for the church-going people of Great Wraggington to work out the right Sunday of the month. On the first Sunday the service was at 10.00 a.m., on the second at 8.30 a.m., on the third at 11.15 a.m., and on the fourth at 6.30 p.m. Phillip imagined that everyone on the parochial church council could have their favourite service time at least once a month.

Phillip opened the church door at about seven minutes past eleven; the door creaked loudly and Phillip walked in. He was surprised just how dark the church was inside, in spite of the bright sunlight outside. The church had been refashioned by the late Victorians in an early English style, making use of very narrow lancet windows, which naturally let in very little light.

To begin with, Phillip could see no-one inside the church at all. Then he saw a man in his late sixties sitting on the organ stool at the back of the church. Phillip sat down in a pew. The organist came forward, switched on the lights and offered Phillip a book and a slim booklet. The dark blue book contained both the *Book of Common Prayer* and the *Standard Edition of Hymns Ancient and Modern*. The pale blue booklet carried the title *Holy Communion in accordance with Alternative Services: First Series*. It was published by the Church Union. Phillip was pleased to think that he would be experiencing a form of service in which he had previously never taken part.

Just before 11.15 a.m., the rest of the congregation arrived, 4 ladies and 2 men, all in their sixties or seventies. Shortly after 11.15 a.m. the clergyman arrived, having come directly from conducting a 10.00 a.m. Communion service in a neighbouring parish. Phillip thought that he looked old and tired, and learned later that he was serving a post-retirement ministry as priest-in-charge of these two small villages. The clergyman went straight across to the organist and began a noisy conversation about the hymns. The organist then came to the front of the church to change some of the hymn numbers, while the clergyman robed in the vestry.

The service began shortly after 11.20 a.m. It was then that Phillip realised that the service was not to be a Communion after all, but something quite different. The vicar came to the front and announced that the service was to be a special Rogation type service, in accordance with local tradition. Phillip wondered what he had let himself in for, and he felt rather disappointed that he was going to miss Communion that day.

The special Rogation type service turned out to be a long, rambling monologue from the vicar, punctuated by five hymns. The hymns were well chosen and Phillip knew them all – 'O Worship the King', 'Through all the changing scenes of life', 'Eternal Father strong to save', 'We plough the fields and scatter', and 'All things bright and beautiful'. The organist played the hymns very slowly and no-one was really interested in attempting to sing them, least of all the vicar. Phillip felt rather self-conscious each time he tried to give a lead.

Phillip found it difficult to follow the point of all that the vicar was saying. He talked about fields and farms and about how things had been in the past, but Phillip did not feel that it was speaking in any way to his experience today. He also found it strange that a whole service should include nothing other than a monologue and hymns. There were no readings from scripture and no prayers. Everything was done by the vicar as a one man show. During the last hymn one of the men from the congregation walked up to the vicar and asked if he should take a collection. Approval was given to this suggestion and a collection was duly taken.

The whole service lasted forty-five minutes. Afterwards the vicar came to the door and spoke to Phillip and to the rest of the congregation as they left. No-one else, however, spoke to Phillip and he felt that the congregation was unfriendly, both towards himself and towards each other. He felt that he had been neither welcomed nor made to feel at home in Great Wraggington church. He went home without any desire to come back on another occasion.

3.30 p.m. Evensong

Hilary chose to attend Evensong at Batsford. Batsford has a reputation in the area for being the last outpost of the tractarian movement. It is a parish which has been lovingly nurtured in the Anglo-Catholic tradition by Father Hastings-Smith for what seems like half a century. Every Sunday this village of 700 inhabitants has a regular pattern of 7.30 a.m. Matins, 8.00 a.m. Holy Communion, 10.30 a.m. Parish Communion and 3.30 p.m. Evensong. Matins, Holy Communion and Evensong were all said on each weekday as well.

When Hilary walked into Batsford church, she felt as if she was stepping fifty years back in time. The church had a clean, newly scrubbed look about it. The brightly polished oil lamps hanging from the tall beams reminded her that electricity had not yet been installed in Batsford church. In a dark corner a solitary candle was burning at the foot of the statue of the Blessed Virgin Mary. She breathed in deeply the aroma of incense and crossed herself at the holy water stoup.

While Hilary was standing by the entrance, absorbing the rich atmosphere, an elderly lady emerged from behind the long blue curtain which sealed off the arch at the base of the tower. She had just finished ringing the angelus. She greeted Hilary warmly and offered her three books, the *Book of Common Prayer*, the *English Hymnal* and a *Manual of Plainsong*. She led Hilary to the front pew and suggested that they should sit together. Then she explained in a loud whisper that she was pleased to be joined at Evensong. Generally she was the only person to come to Evensong these days. She continued to explain that since there is no organist 'we have to sing loudly'.

Father Hastings-Smith had been meditating in his stall for some time before the service was due to start. Just after 3.30 p.m. he stood up and began the office. In spite of the small congregation the canticles and all the psalms set for the day in the *Book of Common Prayer* were sung antiphonally in plainsong chant, the vicar establishing the chant and pitch for each. The office of Evensong was accompanied by the appropriate ritual. During the singing of the office hymn 'The Lamb's high banquet we await' Father Hastings-Smith tottered to the altar, donned a cope and added a fresh supply of incense to the thurible. During the Magnificat both the altar and the congregation were duly censed.

After the third collect, the congregation stood to sing 'Father of heaven, whose love profound', while Father Hastings-Smith moved off to the lady chapel to bring the Reserved Sacrament from the aumbry for Devotions. Returning to the high altar, he led the congregation kneeling in singing the three hymns, 'O Saving Victim', 'O Gladsome Light', and 'Therefore we before him bending'. Devotions closed with the recitation of the Divine Praises and a psalm. The Reserved Sacrament was returned to the aumbry in the lady chapel with due ceremonial. Hilary had not attended a service like this before, and found it rather strange, but she was left in no doubt of either the sincerity and sanctity of the officiant or the willingness of the other member of the congregation to help her find the right place in the hymn book and plainsong manual.

The service lasted for forty-three minutes. Afterwards, Father Hastings-Smith made a special point of welcoming Hilary and of discovering whether she had recently moved into his parish. Hilary felt that Father Hastings-Smith was still taking very seriously his pastoral responsibilities as parish priest, in spite of his great age and the little response he was receiving from his parish in terms of his Evensong congregation.

6.30 p.m. Evensong

For our final experience of the worship of a rural Anglican deanery on the third Sunday in May, we will join Peter as he makes his way to the 6.30 p.m. Evensong in Beckhill. In the early 1950s Beckhill was another country market town which boasted a little industry and about 3,500 inhabitants. During the 1960s and 1970s, the community had expanded rapidly so that today there are over 16,000 people living there.

With the expansion of Beckhill, new shops, factories and offices were built. New schools and community centres were developed on the outlying estates. The Roman Catholic community built a church school and a second church on one of the new estates, and the Pentecostalists and Jehovah's Witnesses started regular meetings in the community centres. The Anglican Church decided to keep all its resources in the medieval church in the centre of the market town. The parish church dominates the town centre and details of the services are all clearly displayed on the large notice board next to the urgent appeal for £45,000 to repair both tower and roof.

By the time that Peter arrived for Evensong there had already been a fair amount of activity in Beckhill church on that Sunday. The day's services had started with an 8.00 a.m. Holy Communion, where there had been a congregation of 9. The main service of the day, the 10.00 a.m. Parish Communion had drawn a congregation of 86. During the afternoon there had been a Sunday School for 10 children and a baptism service. The baptism service nearly filled the church, as six infants had been baptised at the same time, and each infant was supported by a family party.

When Peter arrived he found the church door was open and that a lady in her early sixties was waiting there to greet him. She gave him a warm welcome and handed him a *Book of Common Prayer* and two hymn books, *Hymns Ancient and Modern Revised* and *100 Hymns For Today*. She then showed Peter to a seat. Already Peter was beginning to feel that Beckhill church was a friendly place. Looking round, it seemed to him that the church building itself was well cared for and that people had given a lot of time to the arrangement of the flowers and the polishing of the pews.

Peter had arrived for Evensong quite early, at about 6.20 p.m. While he was waiting for the service to begin he was distracted by a lot of activity in the chancel. Robed members of the choir kept drifting between the vestry and the choir stalls, putting out books, turning pages and talking to each other. Two robed readers appeared at the lectern and noisily discussed which one of them was reading the second lesson and which one was reading the first. The organist came out and put up the hymn numbers, while the vicar talked to him about something else. Peter tried to meditate, but decided that it was a losing battle and so listened to the conversations around him. At 6.25 p.m. the organist began to play, and order was restored to the church. The music was good and Peter began to feel peace return to him.

At 6.32 p.m. the vestry door opened and the choir began to process in. The choir consisted of 11 adults, 2 in their thirties and the other 9 well over the age of sixty. The choir was followed by the two readers, the vicar and his curate. Both clergymen and one of the readers were in their sixties, while the other reader was in his mid-fifties. Once settled in the choir stalls, the choir and ministers seemed very cut off from the congregation by the heavy rood-screen, especially since the readers and clergy sat with their backs to the congregation.

The service was conducted entirely in the chancel, while hardly involving the congregation at all. Both lessons and the intercessions were read by one of the readers. The organ and choir were in good form and sang the psalm, canticles and hymns lustily, but the congregation seemed very unwilling to join in. The four hymns chosen for the service were 'A Man there lived in Galilee', 'Crown him with many crowns', 'Where high the heavenly temple stands' and 'See the Conqueror mounts in triumph'. The choir also sang an anthem, but Peter failed to grasp the composer or the words, since neither of these pieces of information was announced.

Because the anthem had been quite long and so had the intercessions, it was already 7.17 p.m. when the curate mounted the steps to the pulpit to begin his sermon. Evensong was obviously regarded in Beckhill as an opportunity to preach a substantial sermon, and tonight the curate preached for twenty-one minutes. Peter thought that it was really quite a good sermon, although his mind began to wander after the first ten minutes or so. The preacher made good use of personal anecdotes and illustrations, and the sermon was preached generally in simple and direct language. However, it did tend to be dull and elicited no apparent response from the other members of the congregation. Peter thought that it must be difficult to preach to such an unresponsive looking group of people. He also noticed that behind the preacher in the chancel the choir and organist seemed to be busily engaged in their own conversation. The two readers and the vicar continued to sit with their backs firmly towards the preacher.

No collection was taken during this Evensong. During the offertory hymn, Peter suddenly realised that there had been a collection plate by the door as he came in. The welcome which he had received and the way in which he had been shown to a seat had so taken up all his attention that he had failed to put anything into the plate. During the last hymn he watched the lady who had welcomed him to the service take the plate to the altar, and he felt slightly guilty for having contributed nothing to it.

After the service had finished at 7.45 p.m., Peter went up to the bookstall at the back of the church and had a good look at the notice board. The bookstall looked quite interesting, although it was obvious that some of the books had been there for several years: they had developed a faded and rejected appearance. The notice board was not so good. Little care had been taken in putting up notices and several had been left there long after they had become obsolete.

Both of the clergymen were standing by the door to shake people by the hand as they left. The vicar told Peter that it was good to see him in church again, but confessed that he had forgotten his name. Peter felt slightly confused since he had never been there before. He felt that the vicar probably said the same thing to everyone. The lady who had welcomed him when he had arrived also spoke to him again as he went out and expressed the hope that he would come again. Peter thought to himself that he would like to come back to Beckhill church again, but that it would be wiser next time to give Evensong a miss and to try instead the Parish Communion in the morning.

13 DISCUSSION

This study has raised a number of important questions about the situation of the rural Anglican church today. The evidence produced from the three research projects has helped to suggest some answers to these questions, and I have attempted to offer some interpretation of this evidence in the course of my review of it. The real job for evidence of this nature is to stimulate further discussion and to facilitate informed debate. If this research is to be useful, it needs now to be used by the local rural churches themselves and by all of us who share a concern for the life and work of the rural Anglican church, especially as it involved young people.

With this end in mind, instead of ending with a summary of my own conclusions, I have organised a list of the key questions raised by each chapter. My hope is that local churches will be able to use these questions as a vehicle through which to assess their current work and to plan realistically for the future, and that they will want to refer back to the appropriate chapters in order to remind themselves of the kind of evidence available on each issue. In the last analysis, the local churches' responses to these questions will determine whether the research becomes a cause for depression or a springboard for action.

Chapter 1 Introduction

1   What are the implications of the secularization of rural society for the churches?
2   How serious are the effects of decreased resources on the life of the rural churches?

Chapter 2 Historical Perspective

3   How adequate are the statistics assembled by the Church of England to monitor the changes which are taking place?
4   What does the drop in the proportion of the population registered on electoral rolls from 18.7% in 1951 to 7.9% in 1982 say about the changing strength of rural Anglicanism?

5   How can the church usefully respond to the fact that Christmas seems to be taking over from Easter as the main festival for going to church?

6   What are the long-term implications, both positive and negative, for the Anglican Church of the fact that the proportion of infants baptized is decreasing?

7   What are the long-term implications of the drop in confirmation candidates?

8   Is the expansion of lay ministry sufficient to compensate for the reduction in clerical manpower?

9   Is the rural Anglican church making the right use of women in its ministry and leadership?

10   What are the consequences of the reduction in the number of church schools?

Chapter 3 The Survey

11   How difficult is it to maintain a church in a small rural community, or with only a small electoral roll?

12   Does a rural church lose much when it loses its parsonage?

13   How helpful is the development of team ministries in rural areas?

Chapter 4 Head Count

14   How influential is the rural Anglican Church if about 4% of the population attend services or come to other forms of meeting on a typical Sunday?

15   Why does the church have more contact with five to thirteen year olds on Sundays than with older teenagers?

16   What provisions should the rural churches be making for pre-school children and/or older teenagers?

17   What resources do rural churches need in order to work successfully among young people?

Chapter 5 Sunday Services

18   Is rural Anglicanism losing anything valuable by the lack of emphasis placed on the offices of Matins and Evensong?

19   What are the implications of making the Communion the main form of service in rural churches?

20   How helpful are 'Family Services'?

21   How important is the time of day for church attendances?

Chapter 6 From Sunday School to Parochial Church Council

22 What future is there for rural Sunday schools?

23 Is Sunday school work among five to nine year olds useful if the children lose touch with the church after this age?

24 Is the rural church right in opting out of providing youth clubs for non-church members?

25 What kind of provision can the rural church make for teenage church members?

26 Given the large number of children and young people involved in church sponsored uniformed organisations, is the rural church doing enough to foster links with these groups?

27 Given the fact that the majority of confirmands are under the school leaving age, how can confirmation preparation best be arranged for teenagers in a rural area?

28 What part can house groups play in integrating teenage and adult church members?

29 In light of the fact that bell ringing attracts more eighteen to twenty-one year olds than any other church related activity, what can be done to foster links between teenage bell ringers and the worship of the church?

30 Given the ability of church choirs to recruit ten to thirteen year olds, how can this contact be most effectively developed?

31 What can be learnt from the fact that altar serving seems to keep the interest of mid-teenagers better than church choirs?

32 Is enough being done to involve young people on the parochial church councils of rural churches?

Chapter 7 The Clergy

33] zl] How can the clergy make best use of their contact with the uniformed organisations, whether or not church sponsored?

34 How can the clergy make best use of their contact with local primary or first schools?

35 Should the rural church be trying to make more contact with secondary or upper schools?

36 How much should the rural church try to make contact with youth groups it does not directly sponsor?

Chapter 8 Church Growth

37   How helpful are studies in church growth in enabling us to understand the possibilities and limitations facing individual churches?

38   This chapter argues that the most successful rural benefices are those with populations between 1500 and 2500: why should this be the case?

39   Why is it that when electoral rolls grow beyond 150 names, a lower proportion of the number of people on the roll actually seem to attend church?

40   How can we account for the significantly lower level of church attendance in benefices held by clergy over the age of sixty?

41   Why do clergy working in multi-parish benefices have fewer people in their congregation than those working in single parish benefices of the same total populations?

Chapter 9 Church Schools

42   Given the greater contact which the clergy have with church schools than with county schools, should this be taken into account when appointing clergy to benefices which contain church schools?

43   Do clergy need special initial or in-service training for working with church schools?

44   Is it appropriate to expect a church controlled or aided school to produce young church attenders?

Chapter 11 A Deanery in Depth

45   What impression of the life of the Christian community is conveyed by the rural church buildings themselves?

46   How necessary is it to lock rural churches?

47   How can best use be made of church notice boards, parish magazines, and so on?

48   How important is it to display information about the clergy, churchwardens, times of services, etc.?

49   How can newcomers to a church be helped to feel at home and to follow the service?

50 How desirable is it to involve lay people in conducting services, especially those under the age of twenty-two?
51 How important is it to maintain singing in worship when there is a small congregation?
52 Are sermons an effective means of communication for rural churches today?

APPENDICES

APPENDIX ONE –
path analysis

Chapters eight and nine on church growth and church schools have reported the conclusions based on a sequence of path models and multiple regression equations. The aim of this appendix is to present the path models themselves and to discuss their statistical structure in greater detail in order to illustrate the foundations on which the conclusions in chapters eight and nine have been based. All the statistics have been computed by means of the SPSS computer package, subroutine REGRESSION, release 8.1. Full details of the statistical procedures involved, together with an excellent introduction to the theory of path analysis, are provided in the handbooks to this computer package*.

Path analysis employs a system of diagrams to make explicit the assumed causal relationships in multiple regression equations. The diagrams are read in association with regression tables. In these diagrams, the convention is for the direction of the assumed causal relationships to be shown by straight lines and arrow heads. The strength of the relationship is shown by path coefficients, otherwise known as standardised regression coefficients or beta weights. The signs before the path coefficients indicate whether the relationships are of a positive or negative nature. In order to simplify the path diagrams themselves, lines are only drawn when a relationship is statistically significant.

Path model one

The first path model examines the extent to which knowledge about three 'predictors', namely the size of the population, the number of parishes in the benefice and the clergyman's age, can help us to predict both the number of people contacted by the benefices on a typical Sunday and the number of names on the electoral roll. The three predictors are entered into the multiple regression equation in the order

*N.H. Nie, C.H. Hull, J.G. Jenkins, K. Steinbrenner and D.H. Bent, *Statistical Package for the Social Sciences* (second edition). New York, McGraw-Hill, 1975; C.H. Hull and N.H. Nie, *SPSS Update 7–9*. New York, McGraw-Hill, 1981.

PATH MODEL ONE

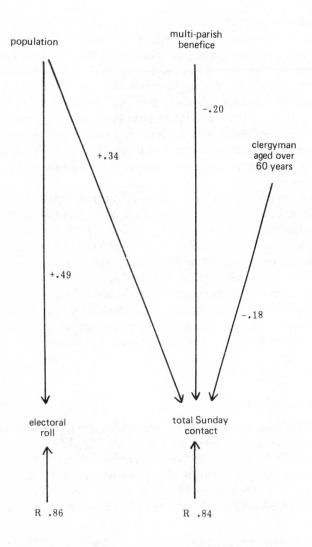

of population, number of parishes and clergyman's age. The lines drawn into the diagram indicate that all three factors simultaneously help to predict the total Sunday contact, while only one predicts electoral roll figures. We shall examine the significance of this in greater detail.

Population is entered into the equation first. The path coefficients show that population is an important predictor of both electoral roll and total Sunday contact, but that it predicts the electoral roll figures more strongly than total Sunday contact. This indicates that recruitment into nominal church membership is more closely related to population size than recruitment into active church membership.

Second, the number of parishes in the benefice is entered into the equation. After differences in population have been taken into account, the number of parishes in the benefice makes no difference to the number of names on the electoral roll, but it does have an effect on the total Sunday contact. If a single parish benefice and a multi-parish benefice of the same population figures are compared, we would expect the combined electoral roll figures for the multi-parish benefice to be roughly the same as the electoral roll figure for the single parish benefice. However, we would still expect fewer people to attend church on a Sunday in the multi-parish benefice. This means that if two clergymen have responsibility for the same number of parishioners, the one who has three churches to look after rather than one will have just as many nominal church-goers on his electoral roll, but fewer active church-goers in his congregations.

Third, the clergyman's age is entered into the equation. After differences in population have been taken into account, and after differences between single parish and multi-parish benefices have been taken into account, the clergyman's age has no effect on the number of names on the electoral roll, but it does influence the total Sunday contact. The path coefficient indicates that the parishes of clergymen over the age of sixty have smaller congregations, although they have the same number of names on the electoral roll. This means that, if two clergymen, one aged fifty and the other aged sixty-five, have responsibility for the same number of parishioners and the same number of parishes, we would expect the older clergyman to have the same number of names on the electoral roll of his churches, but fewer people actually worshipping in those churches on a typical Sunday.

Path model two

The second path model takes the analysis two stages further. First, the

PATH MODEL TWO

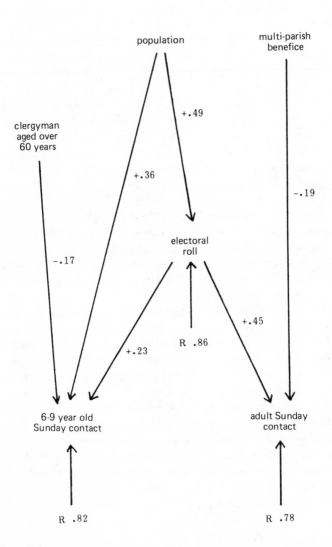

electoral roll is brought higher into the equation. Now electoral roll is seen both as a factor which should be predicted from knowledge of the size of the population, the number of parishes in the benefice and the clergyman's age, and also as a factor which helps to predict Sunday contact, alongside population, number of parishes and clergyman's age. Second, instead of looking at the total Sunday contact of the benefices, path model two looks at two separate notions, the total number of adults and the total number of children aged between six and nine years. The six to nine year olds have been selected for closer analysis because this is the age group with which the rural Anglican churches in the sample have strongest contact. It seemed sensible, therefore, to learn as much as possible from the data about contact with this age group.

What path model two and the statistics in table A1.1 (see page 177) demonstrate is that the churches' contact with six to nine year olds is related to quite different factors from the churches' contact with adults. The only two factors significant in predicting adult Sunday contact are the electoral roll and whether the benefice contains more than one parish. In the case of adult church attendance, the population figures convey no additional information not already communicated from the size of the electoral roll. This means, for example, that if a single parish benefice has an electoral roll of 100, one would expect the same number of adult church attenders, whether the population size is 1,000 or 6,000. At the same time, one would expect a smaller number of adult church attenders in a multi-parish benefice which similarly had an electoral roll of 100 people. In this sense, the electoral roll is a comparatively good index of adult church attendance when used in association with knowledge about whether the benefice contains more than one parish.

On the other hand, Sunday contact with six to nine year olds is related not only to the electoral roll, but also to the population size and the clergyman's age, although it is not related to the number of parishes in the benefice. This means, for example, that if two churches both have electoral rolls of 100 and one of these churches is in a benefice of 6,000 population, while the other is in a benefice of 1,000 population, it is likely that the larger benefice would have contact with more six to nine year olds than the smaller benefice, in spite of the fact that this variation in population size would not be expected to affect the number of adult church attenders.

This indicates that the rural Anglican churches are much more likely to be able to attract the interest of the children of uncommitted parents than the interest of uncommitted parents themselves. The larger the catchment area, in terms of the size of the benefice, the more children of uncommitted parents are likely to come into contact with the rural Anglican church. However, once the adult church congregation has reached its saturation point, the uncommitted parents of these children are not likely to find a place for themselves in the adult worshipping community.

Having constructed path model two, it is now possible to use it to estimate the number of six to nine year olds likely to be contacted by parishes of given characteristics. For example, according to the unstandardised regression coefficients (given a constant of 7.2), we would expect a benefice which has an electoral roll of 100 and a population of 1,000 to have contact on a typical Sunday with 12 six to nine year olds when the benefice is in the care of a clergyman under sixty years of age, and 7 six to nine year olds when the benefice is in the care of a clergyman over sixty years of age. Similarly, a benefice of 6,000, which still had an electoral roll of 100, would be expected to have contact with 18 six to nine year olds if the clergyman was under sixty years of age, and 13 six to nine year olds if the clergyman was over sixty years of age.

Path models three and four

The third and fourth path models, together with table A1.2 (see page 178), were developed by parallel sets of equations to examine the influence of either an aided or controlled church primary or first school on the number of six to nine year olds with whom the benefice has contact. Path model three examines the situation of Sunday contact, while path model four examines weekday contact. Both path models involved precisely the same set of predictor variables, introduced into the equations in the same order. It is for this reason that the differences in the shapes assumed by these two path models is of such interest and importance.

First, electoral roll is regarded as a possible function of the total population of the benefice, the number of parishes constituting the benefice, and the clergyman's age, entered into the multiple regression equation in that order. This equation has already been employed in the earlier path models. Population emerges as an important predictor of the number of names on the electoral roll. The clergyman's age and the number of parishes in the benefice add no significant additional information to the prediction of the number of names on the electoral roll after the size of the population has been taken into account.

Second, the contact with six to nine year olds is regarded as a possible

PATH MODEL THREE

Sunday contact with 6-9 year olds

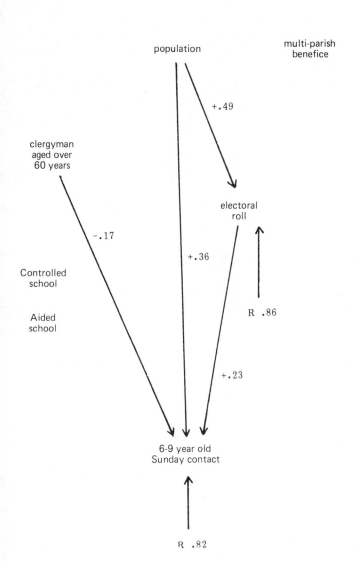

population

multi-parish
benefice

+.49

clergyman
aged over
60 years

-.17

electoral
roll

+.36

Controlled
school

Aided
school

R .86

+.23

6-9 year old
Sunday contact

R .82

PATH MODEL FOUR

Weekday contact with 6-9 year olds

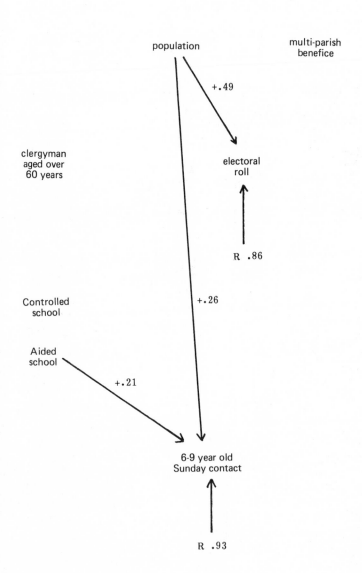

population   multi-parish
                                  benefice

                    +.49

clergyman
aged over
60 years
                          electoral
                          roll

                          R .86

Controlled
school
                    +.26

Aided
school

          +.21

                    6-9 year old
                    Sunday contact

                          R .93

function of the total population of the benefice, the number of parishes constituting the benefice, the clergyman's age, the electoral roll of the benefice, whether the benefice contained a church voluntary aided primary school, and whether the benefice contained a church voluntary controlled primary school. These six predictor variables were entered into both multiple regression equations in precisely the order in which they have been listed above.

Path model three demonstrates that the number of six to nine year olds who come into contact with the church on a Sunday is positively related both to the size of the benefice and the number of names on the electoral roll. The larger the community on which the benefice is able to draw, the more six to nine year olds are likely to come to church or Sunday school. The size of the community is not the only important factor: the number of committed adults on the electoral roll is also important. The adults who are committed to the church are naturally more likely to bring their six to nine year olds with them, or to send them to Sunday school. Path model three also demonstrates that the number of six to nine year olds who come into contact with the church on a Sunday is negatively related to the age of the clergyman. Clergy over the age of sixty have less contact with six to nine year olds on a Sunday.

After all these other factors have been taken into account, path model three demonstrates that the presence of a church school in the benefice, either a controlled school or an aided school, makes no significant difference at all to the number of six to nine year olds who come into contact with the church on a typical Sunday.

Path model four indicates that the number of six to nine year olds who come into contact with the church on a weekday is influenced by quite a different set of factors. The size of the population of the benefice is still the most important factor, but now the number of names on the electoral roll makes no additional difference. The committed church membership does not influence the church contact with six to nine year olds during the week in the same way as it influences Sunday contact.

In the case of predicting weekday contact, the only factor which is important, apart from the number of people living in the benefice and therefore the number of children with whom there is potential contact, is the presence of the church voluntary aided primary or first school. Clergymen who have a church voluntary aided primary or first school in their benefice are likely to make significantly more weekday contact with six to nine year olds, and this is not related in any way to the clergyman's age.

These statistics indicate that the weekday contact between the clergyman and the six to nine year olds is likely to be at the initiative neither of the church congregation nor of the children themselves, but on that of the clergyman making contact with children through school, and the older clergymen are just as likely to persist in making this contact as the younger clergymen. Moreover, the presence of a church voluntary controlled primary school does not function in the same way as the presence of a church voluntary aided primary school. This difference is explicable in terms of the different legal status of the two types of school. Path analysis suggests that the distinction in law is clearly reflected in the clergyman's relationship with the school, and, therefore, with his overall contact with six to nine year olds during the course of the week through the school.

APPENDIX TWO –
tables

My aim in preparing this book has been to include the salient statistical information in the text itself and so to avoid frequent cross-referencing between tables and text. There are just two sets of information which it seems sensible to present more fully than would have been possible in the text itself. Both of these appear in this appendix. Tables 2.1 through 2.5 present in full the historical statistics on which chapter two is based. Tables A1.1 and A1.2 present the full statistical calculations supporting path models two, three and four described in appendix one.

Table 2.1   Population and Electoral Roll 1950 – 1982

Year	Population	Estimated population over 14	Electoral roll	Electoral roll as % population over 14
1950	390754	(299798)	52538	17.5
1956	403190	309340	50500	16.3
1958	409730	314200	52310	16.6
1960	421220	324630	50120	15.4
1962	431280	335720	51061	15.2
1964	441650	343630	49648	14.4
1966	458040	356500	48152	13.5
1968	476490	370050	46570	12.6
1970	486510	376050	45814	12.2
1973	499450	381690	36441	9.5
1976	513329	395385	36097	9.1
1978	528038	411936	30654	7.4
1980	537500	423100	31400	7.4
1982	541000	425700	31200	7.3

Table 2.2   Communicants at Easter and Christmas 1956 – 1982

| Year | Easter (incl. Easter Week) | | Christmas | |
	N	% population over 14	N	% population over 14
1956	33953	11.0	26631	8.6
1958	34376	10.6	27955	8.9
1960	33950	10.5	28624	8.8
1962	36241	10.8	27556	8.2
1964	32959	9.6	27765	8.1
1966	32483	9.1	29473	8.3
1968	30363	8.2	27979	7.6
1970	28623	7.6	25204	6.7
1973	28297	7.4	27004	7.1
1976	28776	7.3	26028	6.6
1978	29385	7.1	28423	6.9
1980	29000	6.9	29200	6.9
1982	29200	6.9	28100	6.6

Table 2.3   Baptisms 1956 – 1980

Year	Infants	Live births	Infants baptised as % live births	All other people
1956	4079	6455	63.2	270
1958	3934	6677	58.9	190
1960	3982	7110	56.0	218
1962	4183	7360	56.8	193
1964	4184	7990	52.4	182
1966	4266	7860	54.3	166
1968	4196	7930	52.9	151
1970	3924	7730	50.8	155
1973	3513	7390	47.5	112
1976	2697	6368	42.4	120
1978	2498	6313	39.6	596
1980	2760	7110	38.8	610
1982	2400	6700	36.6	640

Table 2.4   **Confirmation Candidates 1955 – 1982**

Year	Males	Females	Totals
1955	1689	1303	2992
1956	1121	1211	2332
1957	1556	1179	2735
1958	1631	1272	2903
1959	1658	1341	2999
1960	1569	1336	2905
1961	1572	1367	2939
1962	1473	1316	2789
1963	1333	1116	2449
1964	1174	1088	2262
1965	980	935	1915
1966	922	919	1841
1967	699	951	1650
1968	621	802	1423
1969	749	1058	1807
1970	530	802	1332
1971	511	837	1348
1972	405	684	1089
1973	268	416	684
1974	375	721	1096
1975	440	702	1142
1976	482	665	1147
1977	462	658	1120
1978	489	743	1232
1979	525	630	1155
1980	469	714	1183
1981	476	717	1193
1982	414	587	1001
1983	422	623	1045

Table 2.5   Clergy and Readers 1956 – 1982

Year	Readers	Total full-time diocesan clergy	Clergy:population ratio
1956	117		
1957	117	286	1:1417
1958	146	284	1:1443
1959		288	1:1439
1960	133	291	1:1447
1961		300	1:1386
1962	144	305	1:1414
1963	142	287	1:1523
1964			
1965	148	298	1:1503
1966	149	300	1:1527
1967	144	303	1:1541
1968	143	299	1:1594
1969	152	292	1:1630
1970			
1971	149	288	1:1660
1972	152		
1973	163	262	1:1906
1974	166		
1975	174		
1976	173	222	1:2312
1977	176	205	1:2556
1978	194	211	1:2503
1979	191	204	1:2608
1980	207	208	1:2584
1981	165	206	1:2569
1982	204	207	1:2613
1983	204	212	

Table A1.1: Path model two

Criterion Variable	Predictor Variable	R^2	Increase in R^2	B	Beta	Standard error B	F ratio	df	p<
Electoral Roll	Population	.23814	.23814	+ 1.19538	+.48625	0.18403	42.194	1,162	.001
	Multi-parish benefice	.23830	.00017	+ 3.31349	+.01826	13.56769	0.060	1,162	NS
	Clergy age	.25269	.01439	-23.38138	-.12038	13.23821	3.119	1,162	NS
Adult Sunday contact	Population	.18665	.18665	+ 0.28039	+.12701	0.16820	2.779	1,161	NS
	Multi-parish benefice	.21440	.02775	-30.33982	-.18618	11.04754	7.542	1,161	.01
	Electoral Roll	.37957	.16516	+ 0.40382	+.44967	0.06396	39.861	1,161	.001
	Clergy age	.38968	.01011	-17.76883	-.10187	10.88055	2.667	1,161	NS
6 – 9 year old Sunday contact	Population	.24502	.24502	+ 0.13117	+.35954	0.03006	19.042	1,158	.001
	Multi-parish benefice	.24509	.00007	+ 0.02609	+.00097	1.95931	0.000	1,158	NS
	Electoral Roll	.29263	.04754	+ 0.03386	+.22821	0.01145	8.747	1,158	.01
	Clergy age	.32132	.02869	- 4.76199	-.16520	1.91745	6.168	1,158	.05

NOTES

1. Population rounded to hundreds
2. Benefices dichotomised into single parish and multi-parish benefices
3. Age dichotomised into under sixty-one and over sixty

Table A1.2: Path models three and four

Criterion Variable	Predictor Variable	R^2	Increase in R^2	B	Beta	Standard error B	F ratio	df	P<
Electoral Roll	Population	.23814	.23814	+ 1.19538	+.48625	0.18403	42.194	1,162	.001
	Multi-parish benefice	.23830	.00017	+ 3.31349	+.01826	13.56769	0.060	1,162	NS
	Clergy age	.25269	.01439	−23.38138	−.12038	13.23821	3.119	1,162	NS
6 – 9 year old Sunday contact	Population	.24502	.24502	+ 0.13190	+.36151	0.03002	19.306	1,159	.001
	Multi-parish benefice	.24509	.00007	− 0.01316	−.00049	1.95675	0.000	1,159	NS
	Electoral Roll	.29263	.04754	+ 0.03374	+.22732	0.01144	8.698	1,159	.01
	Clergy age	.32132	.02869	− 4.86182	−.16866	1.91169	6.468	1,159	.05
	Aided schools	.32148	.00016	− 0.95104	−.02206	2.97469	0.102	1,159	NS
	Controlled schools	.32278	.00130	− 1.07359	−.03932	1.94301	0.305	1,159	NS
6 – 9 year old weekday contact	Population	.08052	.08052	+ 0.09604	+.26383	0.03392	8.016	1,159	.01
	Multi-parish benefice	.08135	.00083	− 0.84149	−.03132	2.21111	0.145	1,159	NS
	Clergy age	.08787	.00652	− 2.56718	−.08926	2.16019	1.412	1,159	NS
	Aided schools	.12892	.04102	+ 9.03474	+.21008	3.36136	7.224	1,159	.01
	Controlled schools	.12915	.00023	− 0.40211	−.01476	2.19558	0.034	1,159	NS
	Electoral Roll	.13134	.00219	− 0.00818	−.05523	0.01293	0.400	1,159	NS

APPENDIX THREE –
the rural spectrum

According to a variety of criteria the individual dioceses in the Church of England can be located on a continuum ranging from the most rural to the most urban. On most of these criteria the diocese of Hereford emerges as the most rural, while the dioceses of Birmingham, Liverpool, London and Southwark vie for the position of most urban. The diocese on which the present research was based comes quite close to the rural end of the continuum. The intention of this appendix is to define more carefully its place on this continuum.

Population density is the most obvious criterion. The average population density throughout the 43 English dioceses in 1980 was 918 people per square mile. In Hereford the population density stands at 157, while in London it is 11,503. Our diocese comes eighth in rank order from the rural end of the continuum, with 369 people per square mile.

The size of the individual parishes is a second obvious criterion. In Hereford the average population of each parish is 716 people, compared with 8,004 in Birmingham. Our diocese stands second in rank order after Hereford with an average population of 1,158.

The proportion of the population who attend church or who have their names on the electoral roll is generally higher in rural areas. The area of highest church attendance is the Hereford diocese, attracting 4.6% of the population on a usual Sunday, compared with Birmingham attracting only 1.4%. In our diocese the average Sunday church attendance of 3.8% makes it rank eighth in the league table. Similarly our diocese ranks ninth in terms of the proportion of the population aged over fourteen who receives communion at Easter (6.9%), compared with 11.6% in Hereford and 2.5% in Birmingham. At the same time our diocese ranks seventh in terms of the proportion of the population who are registered on the electoral rolls of the parishes.

In rural areas the number of people within the care of each full-time parochial clergyman is lower, while the number of churches within his care is higher. In the diocese of Hereford each full-time parochial clergyman has care over an average of 3.5 churches, compared with the clergy in the diocese of Birmingham, London and Liverpool who have an average care over only 1 church. The care over an average of 2.5

churches places our diocese fourth in line at the rural end of the continuum on this criterion. In the diocese of Hereford there are 2,090 parishioners for each full-time parochial clergyman, compared with 7,163 parishioners for each full-time parochial clergyman in the diocese of Birmingham. The ratio of 2,728 parishioners for each full-time parochial clergyman places our diocese third in line at the rural end of the continuum on this criterion.

BIBLIOGRAPHY

Beasley-Murray, P. and Wilkinson, A. (1981) *Turning the Tide*, London, Bible Society.

Betton, J. (Chairman) (1981) *Shared Ministry*, Ipswich, Diocese of St Edmundsbury and Ipswich.

Brierley, P. (Ed.) (1980) *Prospect for the Eighties*, London, Bible Society.

Brierley, P. (1983) *Prospect for the Eighties: Volume Two*, London, MARC Europe.

Calvert, I. (Ed.) (1984) *A Workbook on Rural Evangelism*, Guildford, The Archbiship's Council on Evangelism.

Calvert, I. (Ed.) (1984) *A Second Workbook on Rural Evangelism*, Dorchester, Partners Publications.

Carr, W. (1981) *Organising the Ministry of the Church of England in a Rural Context*, Chelmsford, Cathedral Centre for Research and Training.

Clarke, J.E. (1978) *Mission in Rural Communities*, London, Methodist Home Mission Division.

Davies, E. (1979) *The Church in Our Times*, London, Epworth Press.

Dorey, T. (1979) *Rural Ministry*, Oxford, Oxford Institute for Church and Society.

Down, M. (1984) The shape of the rural church, *Theology*, 87, 164–172.

Dow, G., Ashton, P., Gillett, D. and Prior, D. (1983) *Whose Hand on the Tiller?*, Nottingham, Grove Books.

Eaton, D. (1984) Ministry in Surrey Villages, *New Fire*, 8, 203–208.

Edwards, G. (1980) *Rural Mission*, London, Baptist Church House, Mission Department.

Gill, R. (1977) Theology of the non-stipendiary ministry, *Theology*, 80, 410–413.

Hodge, M (1983) *Non-Stipendiary Ministry in the Church of England*, London, CIO Publishing.

Hopkins, S. (1970) *The Rural Ministry*, London, SPCK.

Jewiss, O.R. (Chairman) (1981) *The Rural Face of the Diocese*, Oxford, Diocesan Board for Social Responsibility.

Luke, R.H. (1982) *The Commission of the Church in the Countryside*, London, Chester House Publications.

Morgan, E.R. (Chairman) (1940) *The Church in County Parishes*, London, SPCK.

Mullen, P. (1984) *Rural Rites*, London, Triangle/SPCK.

Musselwhite, M. (Chairman) (1975) *Youth and the Rural Church*, London, Methodist Home Mission Department.

Newton, C. (1981) *Life and Death in the Country Church*, London, Church of England Board of Mission and Unity.

Nott, P. (1978) Teams and groups and their problems, *Theology*, 81, 14–17.

Obelkewitch, J. (1976) *Religion and Society in South Lindsay*, Oxford, Clarendon Press.

Paul, L. (1964) *The Deployment and Payment of the Clergy*, London, CIO.

Paul, L., Russell, A. and Reading, L. (eds) (1977) *Rural Society and the Church*, Hereford, Diocesan Board of Finance.

Ranson, S., Bryman, A. and Hinings, B. (1977) *Clergy, Ministers and Priests*, London, Routledge and Kegan Paul.

Russell, A. (Ed.) (1975) *Groups and Teams in the Countryside*, London, SPCK.

Russell, A.J. (1975) *Village in Myth and Reality*, London, Chester House.

Russell, A. (1980) *The Clerical Profession*, London, SPCK.

Sedgewick, P. (Ed.) (1984) *A Rural Life Reader*, Satley, Northern Institute for Rural Life.

Smith, A.C. (1960) *The South Ormsby Experiment*, London, SPCK.

Thomas, W.J. (1969) Is the vicar dead?, *Theology*, 72, 264–267.

Tiller, J. (1983) *A Strategy for the Church's Ministry*, London, CIO Publishing.

Toon, P. (1984) Preserving medieval churches, *Theology*, 87, 110–113.

Towler, R. and Coxon, A.P.M. (1979) *The Fate of the Anglican Clergy*, London, Macmillan.

Wedderspoon, A. (Ed.) (1981) *Grow or Die*, London, SPCK.

West, F. (1960) *The Country Parish Today and Tomorrow*, London, SPCK.

Wignall, P. (1982) *Taking Custody of the Future*, Oxford, Oxford Institute for Church and Society.